Imperial Cape Cod Glass

Myrna and Bob Garrison

Schiffer Publishing Ltd

4880 Lower Valley Road, Atglen, PA 19310 USA

Dedication

To Lucile Kennedy
To Helen and Bill Clark
To Keith Burkart
To Paul Gould
To Max Miller
To all fellow Cape Cod collectors

And to our special family, Robert and Jenny Garrison; Janna and Kirkby, Kendra, Nathan, Matthew and Scott Townsend

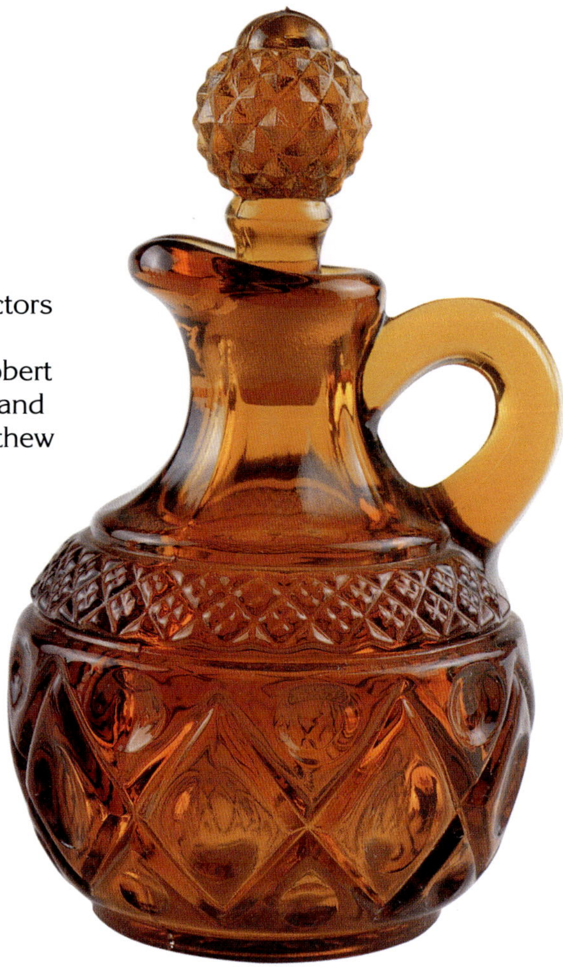

Parts of this book appeared in a slightly different version in *Imperial Cape Cod: Tradition to Treasure,* ©1982, Revised ©1991 by Myrna and Bob Garrison and *Milk Glass, Imperial Glass Corporation, Plus Opaque, Slag and More* © 2001 by Myrna and Bob Garrison.

The authors wish to extend appreciation to Lancaster Colony Corporation for permission to publish photographs and documents of the former Imperial Glass Corporation.

The authors extend appreciation to Ocean Spray Cranberry Company for its aid in trying to help with identifying the purpose of a special order of promotional glass.

All photographs, except Imperial Corporation photographs, were taken by the authors.

Cover photo: 160/246, 7 oz. Square Pitcher, $*; 160/237, Ketchup Bottle, $*; 160/132, 15" Covered Pokal, $135-150; 160/188, 12 oz. Handled Stein, hand painted handle, $*; 160/149D, 8" Center Handled Tray, $115/130.

Library of Congress Control Number: 2003110631

Designed by Mark David Bowyer
Type set in Lydian BT/Korinna BT

ISBN: 0-7643-1953-1
Printed in China
1 2 3 4

Published by Schiffer Publishing Ltd.
4880 Lower Valley Road
Atglen, PA 19310
Phone: (610) 593-1777; Fax: (610) 593-2002
E-mail: Info@schifferbooks.com
Please visit our web site catalog at **www.schifferbooks.com**
We are always looking for people to write books on new and related subjects. If you have an idea for a book, please contact us at the above address.

This book may be purchased from the publisher.
Include $3.95 for shipping.
Please try your bookstore first.
You may write for a free catalog.

In Europe, Schiffer books are distributed by
Bushwood Books
6 Marksbury Avenue
Kew Gardens
Surrey TW9 4JF England
Phone: 44 (0) 20 8392 8585
Fax: 44 (0) 20 8392 9876
E-mail: Bushwd@aol.com
Free postage in the UK. Europe: air mail at cost.

Contents

Acknowledgments

To the Imperial Glass Corporation, which made the wonderful glass that continues to please people long after the factory ceased.

To Lucile Kennedy for helping with the beginning of our research twenty-three years ago. It was that first meeting that started us thinking about sharing facts that we were finding. Thanks for opening the door and keeping it open!

To Helen and Bill Clark for so generously sharing Imperial records, without which this book would not be as complete. Without their friendship and contributions, our research might have stalled.

To Keith Burkart and Paul Gould, two great people who share our interest in collecting Cape Cod. While we compete, each of us is always helping to find the needed pieces for the other's collection. There is first hand sharing of observations. Many pieces of the special Cape Cod photographed for this book were carefully packed by them and brought for the added pleasure of collectors to see and share.

To Max Miller for sharing his expertise on glass in general and Imperial Glass in particular. He is always ready to discuss the differences and similarities of Imperial glass patterns.

To Kathy Burch, our long time Imperial Glass confidant. We have shared finds and observation on all patterns and categories of Imperial glass for twenty years.

To Bev and Jim Harris for the loan of decorated pieces of Cape Cod to be photographed, for helping with the pricing, and for listening.

And to the following dealers and friends who have shown and alerted us to exceptional items to make our Cape Cod collection more complete or contributed in some way to our research: Bill and Margaret Mitchell, Reva Childers, Art and Shirley Moore, Earl and Peggy Thornton, Barbara and Jim Peterson, Diane and Dale Smyser, James McKnight, Joan and Joe Cimini, Willard Kolb, Richard and Wilma Ross, Alice and Bill Starrett, Bob Burns, Kathy Doub, Flo Ross, Crockett Richardson, and all others who have spent their time and effort in finding glass and making it available to collectors like us to be able to buy and enjoy.

To Peter Schiffer for his patience and always positive comments. To Bruce Waters our sincere thanks for his technical advice regarding the photographs. To Mark Bowyer for the great design to highlight Imperial Cape Cod. Last but certainly not least, our sincerest thanks to Donna Baker, our editor, who cheerfully helped us throughout the process of writing this our fourth book for Schiffer Publishing, Ltd. Her suggestions have been a tremendous help and she was always there for us.

Preface

Most collectors are familiar with some patterns of glass for which the Imperial Glass Corporation was famous. However, collectors are not always aware of the amount and the many types of glass that the company produced. In 1978, we became avid collectors of Imperial Glass, particularly the Candlewick and Cape Cod patterns. We made our first trip to the factory in 1980 and wrote our first book, *Imperial Cape Cod: Tradition to Treasure* in 1982. We had already met Mrs. Tommie Carroll, a former Imperial Representative (now deceased), at the Dallas Trade Mart. She was instrumental in our early research by lending us her catalogs and other printed material.

Our interest in Cape Cod came about rather by accident. When we married in June 1948, we received a starter dessert set of Candlewick. About this same time, my mother selected Cape Cod for her stemware and accessory pieces. Eventually those pieces of Cape Cod were ours and we have enjoyed both patterns for years by using them for family dinners and entertaining friends. It is next to impossible for us to talk about one pattern without mentioning and comparing the other.

On that first trip to the factory in 1980, we met Miss Lucile Kennedy, Assistant to the President of Imperial Glass Corporation. Miss Kennedy opened her office and records to us, and thus supplied us with a wealth of data to draw upon in researching our first book. She continues to encourage us in our research.

In the years since 1980, we have missed only one year making a trip to the factory and now to the factory area. In addition, we joined the National Imperial Glass Collectors' Society (NIGCS) and became acquainted with other collectors of Imperial glass. We have made strong and lasting friendships within that group, and the annual NIGCS Convention is a reunion we do not want to miss.

Due to financial hardships, the Imperial Corporation began to sell wares from its archives and basement storage area in 1983. We were fortunate enough to have made several friends among the Imperial employees, and they helped us look into and buy from special reserves. While we were searching in the basement, a friend stepped forward to help us. Helen Clark of the accounting department came down to bring us a flashlight for our hunt. That beam is still burning today as Helen continues to shed light on questions and share factory information with us!

By 1991, we had found many more items of the Cape Cod pattern, and enough material and information to publish a new, revised edition of *Imperial Cape Cod: Tradition to Treasure*. Even as we researched the first Cape Cod book, however, our interest in other Imperial glass began to intensify. Thus, while the updating of the Cape Cod book took precedence, we also made voluminous notes on milk glass production by Imperial, as we searched company records before the 1982 bankruptcy. In 1992, our next book, *Imperial's Vintage Milk Glass*, made its appearance. We believe this book was of interest to both milk glass collectors and Imperial Glass collectors, because many of the six hundred plus molds used to produce milk glass items were subsequently used for many of the beautiful colors that Imperial created.

We had been collecting Candlewick and Cape Cod perfumes and colognes for a long time. Next, we started adding milk glass colognes and found that we were hunting for other Imperial boudoir items as well. We shared our finds with Helen, and discussed with her the relevant facts of each. As always, Helen came to the rescue with pertinent documentation that she had. In 1990, Helen called about the sale of several colognes that Imperial made for Irving W. Rice. Naturally, we bought them. Many items later, we are completely hooked on that area of collecting!

During the years since the closing of Imperial, Helen has shared with us notes and records about the Irving W. Rice Company. In the fall of 1993, we went to the Rakow Library at the Corning Glass Museum to research all the Imperial Glass records. With the help of this material and the invaluable information on the Irving W. Rice card file supplied by Helen, we were able to build a substantial data bank of documented material. The publication of *Imperial's Boudoir, Etcetera . . . A Comprehensive Look at Dresser Accessories for Irice and Others* © 1996 allowed us to share another of Imperial's contributions to the glass world.

Through our collecting years, we have been asked many questions about Candlewick at conventions, shows, meetings, and by telephone and letter. There have been numerous requests made that we write a book on Candlewick—to put our observations and answers into a book for all Candlewick collectors. Finally, we decided to follow some of the urging and coaxing of fellow collectors to write down our discoveries from our Imperial research files and from our personal observations. The result was *Imperial Candlewick, Little Known Facts* ©1999.

Soon we arrived at the need for an updated book on Imperial's milk glass. With our first book on this subject sold out, a few undocumented items to report on, several pieces to photograph that were not pictured previously, and a desire to include the wonderful milk glass boudoir pieces, we decided to undertake a second version of *Imperial's Vintage Milk Glass*. This led to the publication of *Milk Glass, Imperial Glass Corporation, Plus Opaque, Slag and More* (Schiffer Publishing Ltd., 2001).

After the release of our first book published by Schiffer, several friends again started asking for a Candlewick book with photos. As one so aptly put it, "if they [Schiffer Publishing, Ltd.] can make milk glass look that great, just think what they could do to Candlewick." Since our book *Imperial Candlewick, Little Known Facts* © 1999, had sold out, we started thinking about following our hearts and writing a book that included many photographs showing the story of Imperial's most popular pattern, which just happened to be our wedding crystal.

We started making production charts January 1, 2001. In the following summer, we took 1800 slides for the Candlewick project and 900 slides for the Cape Cod project. Taking those slides was a feat that took longer than we anticipated. Again, Helen Clark made factory records available to us. One little mention of a company or an object would take on an important meaning when we would find another mention in another paper. We would move from the card file, to the catalogs, to the price lists, to the memorandums, and back over everything again. More help came when we received word in October 2001 that the factory catalogs and papers that had belonged to Mrs. Tommie Carroll could be ours if we still wanted to buy them. We had waited fifteen years to have the opportunity to own these papers and now they could help fill in gaps with the other materials we had.

In the beginning of writing on Imperial Candlewick, we planned on one book. As the work progressed, we knew that the project was growing more than anticipated. A decision was reached to publish two books, so that no information or photographs would have to be omitted. The first book, *Candlewick: The Crystal Line*, covers all of the general line crystal items. The second book, *Candlewick: Colored and Decorated Lines*, identifies and documents many of the Candlewick colors and decorated items that collectors have puzzled over.

It always seems that when searching through records for information on one pattern, you will see facts about another pattern. As we were working on our two Candlewick books, we could hardly wait to get started on Cape Cod.

As in all of our research, we have used company catalogs to assemble charts of each mold number, with the catalog and price lists in which it appeared for sale. In this manner, we could determine approximately in which year an item was introduced and when it was last cataloged for sale. We feel that these dates of production add a unique facet to a collector's knowledge, and aid in the building of a collection. How long a piece remained in production helps determine a value. Naturally, a piece may have been produced before it was shown in a catalog, just as a piece was usually still available for order after being dropped from the catalog. However, researchers and collectors usually think of production dates as being from the first time an item was cataloged until the last time it was cataloged.

There will always be questions regarding the research methods used in any project. We have tried to deal with catalog facts and not undocumented theories. Our dates were established by using the written material that was available. Due to fewer company catalogs and records before 1950, earlier detailed dates are impossible.

Now we are at the end of this photographic look at Imperial's Cape Cod. We hope that it will help you to know this pattern better and that it will add to your enjoyment of collecting Cape Cod. Whatever your interest is, we hope that our book will measure up to your expectations. It may be a book that you study intently or it may be your wish book. However you use the book ...seek, find, and enjoy.

A Guide To Using This Book

The main purpose of our book about Cape Cod is to help you identify the different pieces of Imperial's Cape Cod pattern. Just as important as identifying the different pieces is knowing the various colors and treatments that are documented for the pattern. Not many pieces of Cape Cod are decorated, but collectors should know all that is possible so they will not pass by an outstanding item when they see one.

Part I of this book provides collectors with a brief history of the Imperial Glass Corporation and the story of Cape Cod. Part II shows the many pieces of Cape Cod made in the crystal line. Color and miscellaneous decorations are shown in Part III, which is a comprehensive effort to list items by color. Part IV provides important information about items for special customers. Part V is filled with undocumented items, whimsies, and Imperial memorabilia. Last is Part VI, covering reproductions and similarities.

It is just as important to read what has been said about the item as well as to study the photographs. We have attempted to put pertinent information in each caption but often much more is needed to tell the story. When necessary, that is presented in the text before the photographs. Remember that when we give a listing of items, we will first list the mold number and then the description. Other information will be included when useful. Occasionally the photograph of a single item will represent other items of the same shape but with different measurements. Do not overlook any of the possible pieces.

Numbering System

When Cape Cod was first introduced in 1931, the numbering system was rather difficult to understand. Several pieces carried the same number with only a letter difference. Eventually, Imperial used the prefix 160/ for most of the Cape Cod line. The numbers to the right of the forward diagonal are numbers assigned by Imperial to specify the particular identification of the individual item. A few times, Imperial changed the identification number during the production years of the piece. This is confusing to researchers and collectors, but it is something that has to be accepted. In presenting the different items, we will generally list them in numerical order according to items within a group. However, there will occasionally be times when we need to place something out of order to keep the visual presentation in the best sequence for comparison. For those items with an early number changing, we have attempted to show both numbers, with the oldest number placed in parentheses. The early numbers are difficult to follow because so many items carried the same or similar numbers. It would be too cumbersome to show every example of the dual numbers so we will try to show them when we think it is best.

There are series of numbers, 1600, 1601, 1602, 3600, and 160, where one number for each design represents all items in that group. The first four groups are comprised mainly of stemware and tumblers. The 160 series has fourteen pieces of stemware as well as being the first three numbers of the identification number used with all remaining pieces of Cape Cod. For ease in conversation, collectors will often refer to an item by dropping the 160, e.g. the 160/210 will be called a 210.

In 1973, when Lenox took control of Imperial Glass Company (see "A Short History of Imperial Glass Corporation"), Lenox changed Imperial's numbering system to a five-digit number. In the table below, the newer Lenox numbers are shown with their corresponding Imperial mold numbers. This is given to aid any collector or dealer attempting to coordinate the Lenox production numbers with the more common identification numbers as used in Imperial catalogs (from which this reference book was assembled).

Lenox	Imperial	Description
16020	160	6 oz. Tumbler
16030	160	7 oz. Old Fashioned
16060	160	10 oz. Tumbler
16090	160	12 oz. Tumbler
16110	160	14 oz. Double Old Fashioned
16120	160	14 oz. Tumbler
16215	160	14 oz. Magnum or Goblet
16200	1602	11 oz. Goblet
16220	1602	6 oz. Dessert
16230	1602	6 oz. Low Sherbet
16240	1602	5 oz. Claret
16300	1602	6 oz. Footed Tumbler
16310	1602	12 oz. Footed Tumbler
16152	24	48 oz. Pitcher
16254	176	5 pt. Pitcher
16360	1D	6 1/2" Plate
16370	3D	7" Plate

16380	5D	8" Plate
16400	10D	10" Plate
16410	145	11 1/2" 2-Handled Plate
16420	75	14" Torte Plate
16435	35	Tea Cup and Saucer
16437	37	Coffee Cup and Saucer
16465	116	Salt and Pepper
16470	117	Salt and Pepper
16475	251	Salt and Pepper
16480	70	Cruet
16490	119	Cruet
16500	76	Coaster
16530	30	Sugar and Creamer
16555	1W	4 1/2" Fruit Bowl
16560	23B	5" Bowl
16563	198	5 1/2" Lug Soup
16566	53X	6" Dessert (Baked Apple)
16570	40H	6" Heart Mint
16572	144	4 1/2" Covered Spider
16580	23/1D	2 pc. Serving Set
16590	56	9 1/2" Relish
16596	55	9 1/2" Oval Relish
16610	161	Oblong Butter
16670	67D	11" Cake Stand
16572	62B	7 1/2" 2-Handled Bowl
16690	145B	10" 2-Handled Bowl
16790	80	5" Tall Candleholder
16800	180/1	Handled Candleholder
16880		4 1/2" Spider Candleholder
16852	150	5 1/2" Ash Tray
16960	180	4 1/2" Handled Server
16990	79	2 pc. Hurricane Lamp
16992	79	Hurricane Shade

Although in some cases they are similar, the Lenox numbers are not to be confused with the early numbers that Imperial used with Cape Cod. For this book, we will not refer to the Lenox numbers in the text and the captions. The early Imperial numbers will usually be in parentheses following a descriptive term.

When a set is composed of two, three, or more pieces, the item number may be a combination of the individual numbers. This is not always the case and can be quite confusing. It increases the challenge of interpreting the information and understanding it—that is a vital part of any research study.

Letter Symbols for Shapes

Imperial used letters after the designated item number for design information. In factory paper, there was a list of "Symbols for Shapes." Not all letters in the list pertained to Cape Cod and some of the needed letters were missing. We are including it anyway because it is part of the Imperial story. Some day you may be studying another pattern and one of the letters will answer a question for you.

A	Round
B	Bowl
C	Crimped
D	Flat plate
E	Turned-up handles or sides
F	Float or shallow bowl
H	Heart or fancy crimp
J	Slight outward roll at top
L	Rolled over and out
N	Slight inward roll at top
R	Rolled over and down
S	Square
TB	Tid bit
V	Plate with cupped edge
X	Not on the symbol's list but is on two items

In looking at the charts and working on this part, we found it interesting that most of the use of the letters occurred in items made in the late 1930s and early 1940s. Fewer letters were used in the later mold numbers and then only when those numbers are sets. We cannot guess at what formula Imperial used in its numbering of items.

Imperial sometimes used different words as names for the same items throughout the seventy-year life of Imperial Cape Cod. It would be difficult to attempt to use all of those names on every item; it would be confusing and cumbersome. Therefore, we will use the name that appeared most often in catalogs that collectors are most likely to see. To explain this further, consider comporte and compote, candlestick and candleholder, partitioned and divided, and nappy and bowl. Imperial also used both the terms "Old Fashion and Old Fashioned," however we have chosen to use "Old Fashioned" in all cases for consistency. Additionally, although in today's usage the word "ashtray" is generally written as one word, we have used it as two words since that is the way Imperial wrote the word in all of its catalogs. We have attempted to project all information as nearly as Imperial did for the sake of Imperial history.

Measurements

Measurements given by Imperial in its description of items sometimes refer to the height and sometimes refer to the width. In building the charts, we have found that some of these measurements changed through the years by a half-inch, inch, and sometimes two inches. On occasion, we have mentioned these changes if it seemed important. Often we have just used a combination of the two sizes given by Imperial, such as a change from 6" to 6 1/2". Everyone must remember that Cape Cod is handmade and therefore the measurements will seldom be exact measurement—that is part of the enjoyment of owning handmade glassware.

The following stem measurements will give collectors a tool to use when trying to determine the identification of a particular tumbler or stem. We are listing the measurements of stems and tumblers by giving the height first and the top diameter second. Remember that we only expect the same error tolerance here as that allowed political analysts—3 to 4%.

Mold	Description	Height	Top Dia.
160	16 oz. Tumbler	6 3/8"	3 3/16"
160	14 oz. Tumbler (if same as 16 oz.?)	6 3/8"	3 3/16"
160	12 oz. Ice Tea Tumbler	5 1/8"	3 1/8"
160	10 oz. Water Tumbler	4 1/8"	3"
160	6 oz. Juice Tumbler	4 3/8"	2 7/8"
160	14 oz. Old Fashioned	3 3/4"	4"
160	7 oz. Old Fashioned	3 5/16"	3 5/16"
160	14 oz. Hoffman House, Goblet, Ivy, Magnum	6 1/2"	3 15/16"
160	8 oz. Goblet, Wafer	5 1/4"	3 1/4"
160B	Stem Cocktail, Wafer	3 1/4"	3"
160	Sherbet, Wafer	3 1/2"	3 1/2"
160	2 1/2 oz. Wine, Wafer	3 7/8"	2 3/8"
1600	12 oz. Footed Ice Tea	6 1/8"	3"
1600	10 oz. Goblet	5 3/4"	3 5/16"
1600	6 oz. Sherbet	4 1/2"	3 1/2"
1600	6 oz. Footed Juice Tumbler	5 1/8"	2 3/8"
1600	3 oz. Wine	4 1/2"	2 1/8"
1600	3 1/2 oz. Cocktail	4 1/4"	2 7/8"
1601	12 oz. Ice Tea Tumbler	5 1/4"	2 7/8"
1601	9 oz. Water Tumbler	4 1/2"	3"
1601	6 oz. Juice Tumbler	3 7/8"	2 1/4"
1602	12 oz. Footed Ice Tea	6"	3 1/4"
1602	10 oz. Footed Tumbler	5 5/8"	3 1/8"
1602	11 oz. Goblet	6 1/4"	3 3/8"
1602	9 oz. Luncheon Goblet	5 1/2"	3 1/4"
1602	6 oz. Low Sundae	3 3/4"	3 3/4"
1602	6 oz. Tall Sherbet or Saucer Champagne	5"	3 3/4"
1602	6 oz. Footed Juice Tumbler	5 1/8"	2 5/8"
1602	4 oz. Oyster or Fruit Cocktail	3 5/8"	2 7/8"
1602	5 oz. Claret or Wine	5 1/2"	2 3/4"
1602	3 1/2 oz. Cocktail	4 5/8"	3 1/8"
1602	3 oz. Wine	4 3/8"	2 3/8"
1602	6 oz. Parfait	5 7/8"	2 1/2"
1602	2 1/2 oz. Sherry	4 5/8"	2 1/2"
1602	1 1/2 oz. Cordial	3 1/2"	2"
1602	12 oz. Footed Ice Tea, Concave Stem	6"	3"
1602	6 oz. Footed Juice Glass, Concave Stem	5 1/8"	2 5/8"
1602	4 oz. Oyster or Fruit Cocktail, Concave Stem	3 1/2"	3 1/4"
3600	11 oz. Goblet, Blown	6 5/8"	3 5/16"
3600	6 oz. Sherbet, Blown	4 7/8"	3 5/8"
3600	12 oz. Ice Tea Tumbler, Blown	6 3/8"	3"
3600	6 oz. Juice, Blown	5 3/8"	2 5/8"
3600	5 oz. Wine, Blown	5 3/8"	2 5/8"
3600	4 oz. Cocktail, Blown	4 1/2"	3 1/8"
3600	1 1/2 oz. Cordial, Blown	3 7/8"	1 5/8"
3611	5 oz. Tumbler	4"	2"
3612	12 oz. Tumbler	5 3/8"	2 5/8"
160/153	3 pc. Icer Set, 3 Wedges	2 1/4"	5 3/8"
	Tumbler, 5 1/2 oz. #530	3 1/2"	2 5/8"
	Sherbet or Fruit Lining #530	2 5/8"	3 1/2"
160/188	12 oz. Handled Stein	4 5/8"	3 3/8"
160/250	Bouillon Cup	1 3/4"	3 7/8"
160/225	Egg Cup	4 11/16"	2 3/4"

Dates

The first date used with each item indicates the first catalog or price list that we have in our research materials in which the item appeared. The second date used is the last catalog in which the item appeared. The dates between 1931 and 1953 were obtained in this manner. Any dates between 1953 and the present were obtained similarly and were also verified by the Imperial card file; they are considered as accurate as possible. The 1953 card file contains the only existing written numerical record and was started in 1953 by Miss Kennedy.

Our resources for the 1930s are very limited and sometimes undated, and therefore, any dates involving that period are subject to challenge. These are listed as 1932, which is the date Cape Cod was patented. Occasionally dates for sets will differ from dates of the individual items. This is because Imperial did not always offer the items as sets in the same catalog as the individual items.

The dates—when an item was introduced and when it was dropped from production—are guides to how difficult an item will be to find. The shorter the production time, the more difficult it will be to find a certain item. A brief production time will also greatly influence prices. Another factor in scarcity is whether an item would have been used in groups of six, eight, or twelve for a table setting versus a pitcher, large platter, or any item for which only one would be necessary. Try imagining a piece that you truly desire and see if it is one of those items that a household would only acquire one of—it really makes a difference in the scarcity of a particular item.

There are some instances when an item was discontinued and then was reintroduced later. If an item in the price guide or the illustration section has two sets of dates, the first set of dates indicates when the item was introduced and discontinued and the second set shows when it was reintroduced.

Items Without the Usual Characteristics of Imperial Cape Cod

There are three main identifying characteristics of the Imperial Cape Cod design. They are the recessed circles or thumbprints, the large recessed diamonds around the circles or thumbprints, and the small diamond point band close to the outer edge of an item. Below is a list of some of the pieces that do not have all of the three characteristics and could be overlooked by collectors.

160/61	Individual Salt, no diamond points
160/78	Round Coaster, raised circles, no diamond points
160/85	Square Coaster, flat circles, no diamond points or depressed large diamonds
160/34	Individual Butter, no depressed large diamonds
160/76	Round Coaster with Spoon Holder, raised circle, no diamond points
160/455	Square Tray, diamond points in center
160/183	Mint/Nut Dish, no diamond points
160/184	Mint/Nut Dish, no diamond points

Some of the more unusual items:

1601	Barrel Tumblers
1602	2 1/2 oz. Sherry
160/12	Crescent Plate
160/53/3	3 pc. Icer
160/100	2 Lite Candleholder and Ornament
160/123	Toast and Cheese, Covered
160/149D	8" Center Handle Tray
160/175	Saucer Candleholder
160/190	Sugar & Cream
160/191	Celery Dish, partitioned 1/3, 2/3
160/195	Cookie Jar
160/219	Salt Dip, Pepper and Spoon
160/211	Salt Tray
160/237	Ketchup, Wooden Lid & Metal Lid
160/247	Salt and Pepper
160/250	Bouillon Cup
160/2701	2-Tier Tid Bit, Wooden or Metal
1600	Salt Spoon
1602	11 1/4" Footed Oval Compote, 6 1/2" tall
1608X	11 1/2" Fruit Bowl
3600	Blown Stems
16010R	13" Center Bowl
16880	Spider Candleholder (Lenox Era 1974-1975)

Glass Making Definitions

Here we will attempt to explain one feature that puzzles all collectors. Items sometimes have a raised ridge on the underneath of the piece. Some of the same pieces will not have this but instead will have a ground and polished bottom. When the items have the extra ridge of glass that one can take hold of, it is called a marie. A marie is found on a snapped-up item. In contrast, a ground and polished item has been "stuck-up" on a puntie rod. According to *A Consumer and Retail Guide to Handcrafted Glassware*:

> To fire polish and/or change the shape of an item, it is attached to one of two types of rod-like iron tools: a "puntie" or a "snap." The face or surface of a puntie is red hot, and newly formed glass will easily attach itself to the hot iron [hence the term, stuck-up].
>
> A snap, however, is a long rod with moveable jaws on one end. The jaws on the snap open up to grip the glass item. After being mounted on a snap or puntie, the glass item is placed into a small furnace called a "glory hole." The item heats up, becomes quite soft, and must be spun to maintain its shape. The "finisher" now shapes the item with a charred wooden tool. Oak or apple wood is used, since neither contains rosin, which could seriously mark the glass.
>
> Fire polishing is done for two reasons: first, to give the surface of the glass a higher brilliancy, and second, to soften the glass if it requires a final shaping.
>
> **Finishing**
>
> After finishing, the item is detached from either the snap or the puntie, and placed in a Lehr (annealing oven) to be tempered. Snapped-up items require no further processing after annealing, while items stuck-up must be ground and polished after annealing to remove any rough edges remaining on the foot or base of an item that has stuck to the puntie.

"Crack off" is the excess glass that every piece of blown ware has. An item must be shaped so that it can be inflated to completely fill the mold and assume the proper shape. After annealing, it is necessary to "crack off" the unwanted cap or top portion of the glass. The glass is scored by a wheel, then a hot flame is applied to the scored mark and the unwanted glass will crack off along the scratch. The resulting rough edge is sharp and uneven and must be ground smooth.

Sometimes the marie bottom of an item was the early design, on other items the ground and polished bottom was the early version. It cannot be stated, therefore, that marie bottoms all represent the early style. The only time that Imperial indicated the ground and polished bottoms in price lists was on plates. Marie bottoms were not specifically mentioned.

Here are some answers to often-asked questions:

"What is the difference between blowing and pressing glass? Blowing, the oldest method of forming glass, is done with the aid of an iron blowpipe used by a skilled glass worker. Molten glass is gathered on the end of a blowpipe; it is then removed from the glass pot somewhat cooled, carefully shaped, and then the glob of glass is blown (by means of the mouth and lungs) into a hollow body. The blower shapes the glass bubble further, and in most cases, blows it into the shape in the mold."

"Hand pressed glassware is distinguished from blown glassware by the fact that in pressing, both the inside and outside surfaces of the article are formed and shaped by a mold, the pressure being exerted by an iron former or plunger instead of just lung power alone, as in blowing. A pressed article can be finally hand shaped in the same manner as a blown article, by a skilled finisher using wooden, carbon, or other types of hand tools" (Imperial factory notes).

What is a pokal? The dictionary defines a pokal as a mug, jug, or jar; a vessel for cooling wine or water; a large, usually covered, goblet typically made of glass or silver. A nappy? It is a shallow open serving dish sometimes having one handle. Comporte? A bowl shaped dish with a stem or foot, sometimes with a cover for holding fruits or sweets. A spider? A cast iron fry pan. (In the case of Cape Cod, it would be the glass shaped as a fry pan.)

Why does some Cape Cod have a yellow tinge to it? We have been told that it was due to the chemical mix of the dry ingredients used for making the glass. This seems to be most prevalent in the wafer stemware, which would indicate that it happened in the older glass. Another common occurrence of the yellowish color appears in the baked apple, an item that dates back to the 1930s.

The following question and answer was found in factory notes: "*Is Cape Cod dishwasher safe?* Imperial glass can be cleaned in an automatic dishwasher. *However*, like all fine glass, its brilliancy will eventually become dulled by the detergent. Hand-wash glass in clean, pleasantly hot water and light suds. A little water softener in the water will add to the item's brilliancy. Never use strong soaps or scalding water on decorated crystal."

Pricing

The prices in this book are just a guide. The prices were compiled by using prices seen on pieces for sale in antique malls, shops, shows, and similar places in various locations. The prices do not reflect those very good low prices you find in those fun to search places nor do they reflect the exaggerated high prices that are sometimes seen in auctions of any type. The prices reflect what a knowledgeable buyer will pay a knowledgeable seller for an item. We say, "Judge a price by demand, desirability, and the availability."

In all pricing, we have shown an asterisk (*) if there has not enough activity on an item to establish a guide. Sets are not always the sum of the parts. Since individual prices are given in the captions, the prices of component parts of the sets will not be listed again.

We would like to emphasize that, "It is our theory that if a collector studies and knows what Imperial Cape Cod *is*, then what is *not* Imperial Cape Cod will take care of itself." Every collector should have all available resources to make himself or herself as knowledgeable as possible.

A price guide is not intended to set prices. Neither the authors nor the publisher assume any responsibility for losses that might be incurred by the use of the price guide.

Cardboard display sign provided to retailers of Cape Cod glass, $25-35.

Part I: Historical Perspective

A Short History of The Imperial Glass Company

"Pride of workmanship, skill, and a deep devotion to quality were the prime motivators of Imperial's glassworkers."

A group of investors organized the Imperial Glass Company in 1901. After a period of "several years of construction, installing furnaces, and creating a number of initial moulds," the first Imperial glass was produced in 1904 in Bellaire, Ohio.

Imperial's earliest production was clear pressed glass. Sales were made to the five and dime stores for items such as covered butter dishes, berry bowls, and pickle dishes. These lines expanded into lampshades, jelly glasses, pitchers, salt and pepper shakers, sugars and creamers, and other similar types of glass.

This photograph of the Imperial Glass Corporation was taken just before the razing of the factory.

Artist's drawing of the Imperial Glass Corporation, Bellaire, Ohio.

The period of 1910 to 1929 saw several new Imperial lines. First was Nuart iridescent ware. In this group were the colored and frosted electric lamp shades in an imitation "Tiffany" style. Following Nuart, Imperial introduced Nucut Crystal, which was a handpressed reproduction of English cut glass. (Collectors Crystal was a reintroduction (1950s) of the Nucut and was one of Imperial's most popular giftware lines.)

"Imperial Jewels . . . exquisite freehand iridescent 'stretch glass' items" were introduced in 1916. This was a "high point" of Imperial's production that involved many shops making pressed wares as well as blown and freehand ware.

From 1904 to 1922, the company flourished, though the market changed as machine made glassware came to the forefront. In 1922, the mass-produced glass markets caused Imperial to try new ideas, including the creation of Imperial's "Art Glass," an innovation that proved to be unsuccessful.

In 1929, the forces of the Depression, combined with further loss of major markets, forced Imperial to enter bankruptcy. The company continued operations while in receivership, and with an order from Quaker Oats Company in 1931 for a premium to be packaged in its product, Imperial was able to stay in business. The company was reorganized and named the Imperial Glass Corporation.

The Quaker Oats premium was the forerunner of today's Cape Cod pattern, a line that survived until the demise of Imperial in 1984. Another jewel to continue until the closing in 1984 was Candlewick, a pattern that was introduced in 1936. Candlewick contained the largest number of items in any Imperial line. It eventually became more popular than the earlier favorite, Cape Cod.

A 1930s catalog pictured thirty pieces of opal glass at this time. According to the only 1930s price list available, Imperial produced twenty-four pieces of opal glass in 1932. These are the earliest company documentations found of milk glass produced by Imperial Glass Company. The height of milk glass production of approximately six hundred items was in the 1950s, with production falling off to less than forty items made after 1970. February 1, 1951, was the introduction of the famous superimposed IG hallmark that was in use for twenty-three years. This mark is often found on Imperial milk glass items.

Imperial had many private mold customers. Companies and individuals brought their molds to Imperial for glass items to be specially made. Imperial also supplied items from its own lines to many different distributors and private mold customers, who then added decorations and marketed these items under their company's name. A few of these companies were Sears Roebuck Inc., Butler Brothers, Lightolier [Lighting] Company, Keystone Silver, Inc., Midwest Chandelier Company, Oneida, Ltd., and Irving W. Rice, Inc.

At the beginning of World War II, changes began taking shape in imports. American companies could no longer import glass products from European countries. Irving W. Rice, New York, was a major importer of colognes and powder boxes. With the onset of the war, Irving W. Rice turned to Imperial Glass Corporation to supply the dresser items for which I. Rice was so well known. The year 1939 was the beginning of a long, strong relationship between the two companies that continued through the 1940s. Correspondence in the late 1960s suggested that the two companies were attempting to resume relations. However, in 1973 when Lenox took control of Imperial Glass Corporation, all private mold work was ceased.

Imperial began acquiring glass companies in 1940. The first purchase was Central Glass Works (1940), followed by the purchase of the molds of the Heisey Company (1958). Two lines from the Heisey Company became strong Imperial lines. Heisey Provincial and Old Williamsburg were produced by Imperial in crystal as well as colors. The purchase of Cambridge Glass Company (1960) added Rosepoint and a strong line of candelabra.

World War II and the postwar period were the boom years of Imperial's production. Not surprisingly, the peak of production of Cape Cod and Candlewick was reached and sustained during this time. Contributing to this success were the countless thousands of households being established by young families after the war, and the prosperous American economy that followed.

In 1972, seeing the need for capital investment, Imperial stockholders arranged a stock exchange with Lenox Incorporated. This was accomplished on December 29, 1972, and in 1973, Lenox began marking Imperial glass with an "LIG" mark. In June 1981, Arthur Lorch, a private investor, bought the company from Lenox. The new mark, "ALIG," began appearing in 1982 and was used only during that year. In the fall of 1982, Lenox foreclosed on its note with Mr. Lorch.

Mr. Robert F. Stahl, Jr., a management consultant, bought the company in late 1982 and filed for Chapter 11 bankruptcy to reorganize the company. A small amount of glass produced carried the NI mark for "New Imperial." The last day of general production was June 15, 1984. Appropriately, the last item off the production line was a four-inch swan with 6-15-84 in raised numbers on the inside. In August 1984, after all efforts failed, liquidation was ordered. Consolidated Liquidation Company and Lancaster Colony combined to buy the assets of Imperial Glass Corporation and went on to sell the last remnants of the bankrupt business. Liquidation of Imperial Glass Corporation was completed with the sale of the building to Mrs. Anna Maroon in March 1985.

The molds were sold individually and in groups of varying sizes. Some went to Mexico and others went to Germany. Indiana Glass Company, a subsidiary of

Lancaster Colony, kept the Cape Cod and Old Williamsburg molds. In November 2002, Indiana Glass Company closed and we do not know what the disposition of those molds has been.

Imperial did not mark Cape Cod. It carried a paper sticker in the familiar blue and silver with the words "Handcrafted, Imperial, USA" and the outline of a stem glass. The edge of the oval sticker is scalloped and we recently learned in company papers that this scalloped edge was called the French Edge.

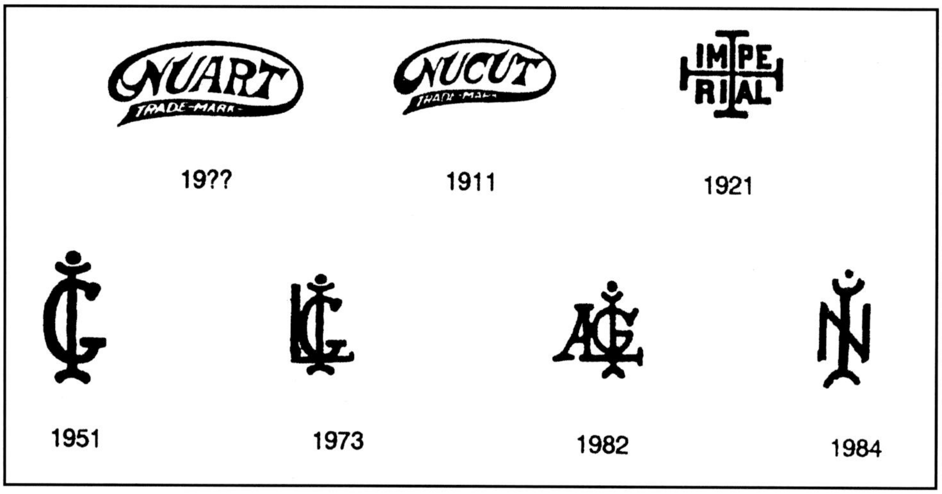

The marks above are those used by the Imperial Glass Corporation. The dates are the dates when the marks were registered or are generally accepted as first used. We do not have registration records for Nuart, but it preceded Nucut.

Mrs. Maroon invested much time and money trying to find a business to occupy the defunct Imperial factory building. It was her desire to provide an economic stimulus to Bellaire, Ohio, and at the same time preserve the historical building that meant so much to so many people for many years. The anchor of this endeavor was the Imperial Hay Shed. Originally, the Hay Shed had been the storage place for hay used in packing glass to be shipped. During the later years, the Hay Shed was an outlet for research and development pieces and factory seconds. From 1985 to 1995, the Hay Shed was an Imperial glass consignment shop that was often the first stop for collectors attending the annual convention of the National Imperial Glass Collectors' Society.

The Bellaire Glass and Artifacts Museum played a vital part in drawing visitors to the partially renovated factory building. There were other tenants, but not enough to fulfill the dream of saving the Imperial Glass Corporation factory building. The building was razed in June 1995 and the Hay Shed outlet was moved to a building on adjacent property. On the ground where the Imperial Glass Corporation once stood, now stands a shopping center. Covering the area where collectors once spent hours and days searching for shards and reminiscing about the greatness of Imperial glass is a blacktop parking lot.

We wrote in our first book ". . . as collectors of Imperial Glass, we have a strong feeling that Imperial will never lose it identity as a producer of fine crystal. In a mass production world, 'Imperial continues to create only handcrafted glassware. Pride of workmanship, skill, and a deep devotion to quality are the prime motivators of Imperial's glassworkers.'" With the close of Imperial, this should be restated: "Imperial continued to create only handcrafted glassware. Pride of workmanship, skill, and a deep devotion to quality *were* the prime motivators of Imperial's glassworkers."

Quoted parts of this history have been condensed from *A Consumer and Retail Guide to Handcrafted Glassware*, by Imperial Glass Corp. Remaining information was obtained through printed information from old records of the Imperial Glass Corporation.

The Cape Cod Story

In the first edition of our book, we stated, "That beautiful Imperial Glass Company's sleeper is waking up. Taking its rightful place among the popular patterns for today's collector is Imperial's Cape Cod pattern. Dealers no longer tell the customer that they are not familiar with the pattern when asked if they have any Cape Cod. New collectors would be wise to choose Cape Cod to collect because it is beautiful, serviceable, and reasonably valued." Today we would have to say that Cape Cod is wide awake.

"Years ago an old, blown, goblet of the shape, size and pattern of today's genuine Cape Cod goblet came into Imperial ownership. Supposedly, Sandwich Glass Company in the New England Cape Cod country had tried to do a pressing based on this superbly fine English article. About 1930, Imperial succeeded where Sandwich had allegedly failed and American Handpressed Cape Cod was born!" This was the way it was told in *Americana Cape Cod, Patterned Glass*, a pamphlet published by Imperial Glass Corporation in 1966, and the way we wrote it in the original edition of this book.

A piece of Cape Cod history was found in some old papers during the liquidation of Imperial Glass. It reads: "The pattern [Cape Cod] was originated in Ireland by the Waterford Glass Company during the sixteenth century and was designed to go with Spode and Wedgwood earthenware patterns. Cape Cod Crystal was the first pattern made by the Sandwich Glass Company of Cape Cod, Massachusetts. When Sandwich went out of business, Pairpoint Glass Company of New Bedford, Massachusetts acquired all rights for hand-cut as well as pressed Cape Cod. They continued making only the hand-cut Cape Cod until 1926 when Pairpoint dropped the hand cut lines. In 1931, Imperial started production of Cape Cod Crystal. This pattern has been sold continuously for nearly 400 years."

The hand cut pattern produced by Pairpoint was called Adelaide. It is a beautiful quality of crystal with a hand cut design with all the characteristics of the Imperial pressed design. Now you can understood the meaning of the statement that one is a collector of "old Cape Cod." Pairpoint's Adelaide pattern will be pictured in the Similarities section on page 149.

For those still not familiar with the beginning of Imperial's Cape Cod pattern, it was introduced in 1931, when—as noted earlier—the sale of five train carloads to the Quaker Oats Company saved Imperial from its first bankruptcy. The pattern is distinguished by three characteristics: a combination of large depressed circles or thumbprints surrounded by a large depressed diamond with an outer band of small diamond points.

Through the influence of Earl W. Newton (Imperial Glass Company President, 1931-1940), Imperial applied for a patent on Cape Cod in 1931 and thus acquired all rights to it in 1932. Three patents were secured at this time and include these patent numbers: 86,626, 160 Ice Tea Tumbler; 86,627, #1604 1/2X Baked Apple Dish; 86,628, #160 Footed Sherbet. In the Imperial files was this statement to all salesmen: "Coverage by patent rights is fairly broad and sizes of articles are not considered. Therefore, all sizes of Cape Cod line, the goblet and other stem pieces are protected by our patent on the sherbet, etc."

There were five items included in the advertising for the Quaker Oats Company premium. This was indicated on the only oatmeal box we have ever seen. These five items included: 160/3D, 7" Plate; 1604 1/2X [160/53X] Baked Apple; 160 Goblet; 160 Sherbet; 160B Stem Cocktail. In the early 1930s, twenty-seven different pieces of Cape Cod were made. One hundred-eighty pieces were being produced at the height of Cape Cod popularity in 1948 and sixteen items were in the 1982-83 catalog when Imperial went into its final bankruptcy. There have been over three hundred pieces and sets designed.

The original Cape Cod stems had a wafer midway in the stem. The 1942 catalog was the last time the wafer stem was shown. Introduced in this catalog was the fancy stem that is often called the miter, strawberry, or pineapple stem.

The advertising writers said it well when they wrote "Tradition to Treasure" in the April 1942 issue of *House Beautiful*. The advertising also commented that "There are more than 100 pieces from which to make your choice." However, our research from a 1942 catalog shows only 78 pieces or sets at that time. This would indicate that the company had available more items than those shown in the current catalog. In addition, price lists contained items not shown in the corresponding catalogs. This might have been accounted for by small quantities of discontinued items.

Other advertisements appealed to the holiday hostess or "to men who might have a penchant for poker"; some even offered a "panacea for coping with the day." A *House Beautiful* advertisement for December 1945 stated, "Every piece of Imperial's scintillating Cape Cod hand-crafter crystal is a gem! This Yuletide choose it only for your discriminating friend." "Pattern for Pleasure," in *House Beautiful* June 1946, offered "Cape Cod Crystal for the gay, informal settings that somehow go with sunshine and a garden full of flowers."

Cape Cod was made for men as well as for the ladies. In *House Beautiful*, September 1946, we find "Aces with Men, Too! . . . That real man's lunch is really 'aces wired' when it's served on Cape Cod Crystal . . . the royal flush of glassware where men are concerned." September 1957 boasts a "...pattern that adds to the blithe spirit of camaraderie wherever gather people of good taste." October 1947 challenges, "Sportsman's Favorite...Bringing home prize pieces of Imperial Cape Cod Crystal is as thrilling to a woman as the bagging of prize game is to the sportsman." It is the same today when bringing home a new *find* for your collection...indeed a prize!

Today, these advertisements could read the same way—Imperial Cape Cod is still the beautiful pattern it was in the beginning. To fully appreciate the well-designed look of Cape Cod, one has only to see a full table set with the pattern or view a buffet serving table resplendent with beautiful Cape Cod accessory pieces. Wait until you see a table accented with Cape Cod in colors; it is breathtaking. Today, Imperial Cape Cod is awake and waiting for the collecting world to enjoy this fabulous pattern in all of its elegance.

Postscript: A new piece of information in the story of Cape Cod was received just as this book was going to the publisher after final proofing. We have just learned that all molds previously owned by Indiana Glass, including those for Cape Cod, were sold to another glass company. Trucks have already dumped unusable molds at a salvage plant. Collectors should be alert to any unusual colors of Cape Cod that may be offered for sale. Reproductions are not necessarily undesirable, but collectors should not pay a high price thinking they are buying an item in a rare, undocumented color. Reproductions in crystal could also appear in the marketplace.

Front cover of 1947 Imperial Cape Cod catalog.

Part II: Crystal Line of Cape Cod

Place Settings

Stemware, Tumblers

160 Series: 1932-1983

Some items in the 160 series of stems and tumblers were in the line from 1932 until 1983. The wafer stem on the 160 series of stems tells you that these are the early design that stayed in the line until late 1942, when the wafter was replaced by the fancy stem discussed in the 1602 series. The 160 series includes the 8 oz. Goblet, Low Sherbet, Stem Cocktail, and 2 1/2 oz. Wine. All are lighter weight and more delicate than their successors in the 1602 line. This is particularly true of the 160B Cocktail. These four can be found in ruby, Ritz Blue, and amber.

Hoffman House is the name of a line of stemware that Imperial made in various colors during the years of production. It is simply a heavy rounded bowl or goblet shape with no pattern on the surface. Several sizes were made for the total line. Only the 14 oz. size was given the name Hoffman House Beer Goblet in the Cape Cod pattern.

After twenty-five years of searching and researching, we feel that there is no difference in the 160 Hoffman House Beer Goblet, Magnum, Goblet, or Ivy except perhaps in the hand finishing of the top rim. The catalog picture of the Hoffman House is just a little different (Hoffman House looks a tiny bit tipped in at the top edge) from the Magnum, Goblet and Ivy, but we think that is because the catalogs are drawings. Yes, we do have some of those with the minute variation, but we think that is only because of the era or the craftsman. The Goblet can be found in Crystal or Evergreen. Our Evergreen Goblet looks more like the drawing of the Hoffman House but the dates for Evergreen (1953-1955) do not substantiate this. It is our strong opinion that all of the 14 oz. Goblets are intended to be the same size and shape. Remember these are handmade objects.

The 16 oz. Tumbler (1953-1973) and the 160/14 oz. Tumbler (1974-1979) have long been a mystery. It seems that all the tumblers we have measured are 15 oz. Since the 16 oz. was dropped in 1973 and the 14 oz. started in 1974, it seems logical that they are the same tumbler that was simply given a better description. When we found our 160 Evergreen Tumblers, we thought we would finally be able to determine the accurate size. The Evergreen tumblers are listed as 16 oz. but guess what? They measure 15 oz. That gives more support to the idea that the 14 oz. and 16 oz. are the same tumbler. Imperial measured by filling items to the top rim.

Everyone loves a story: Collector friends attended a tent sale of movie property in the Kansas City area and found the 160, 10 oz. Water Tumbler shown here, along with this note: "The attached tag certifies that this item was used in Ang Lee's production of 'Ride With the Devil.'" The movie was filmed in the Kansas City area during the summer of 1998 and was scheduled to be released in April 1999. Not being movie buffs, we are unsure if the tumbler was seen in the movie.

160, 14 oz. Tumbler, $25-40; 160, 12 oz. Ice Tea Tumbler or Hiball (1932-1983), $12-15; 160, 10 oz. Water Tumbler (1940-1979), $12-18; 160, 6 oz. Juice Tumbler (AKA Gingerale), $12-15.

160, 8 oz. Goblet, $10-12; 160 Low Sherbet, $10-12; 160B Stem Cocktail, $12-15; 160, 2 1/2 oz. Wine, $12-15. All have the early wafer stem (1932-1943).

The 160, 7 oz. Old Fashioned produced from 1932 until sometime around 1969 has straighter sides than the Old Fashioned produced from 1969 until 1978. In the 1971 catalog, the Old Fashioned has slanted sides with a slight ridge at the base. The #701 Reeded Muddler was used with the Cape Cod 160 Old Fashioned.

The differences in design are important if you are searching for a complete set of this tumbler. This change does not show in any catalog pictures. Since the ruby and Ritz Blue Old Fashioneds do not have the base ridge, and since these colors were produced in the 1930s, it can be safely assumed that the Old Fashioneds with the straighter sides are the early version and the ones with the base ridge are the later style.

A comparison of the early and late versions of the 160, 7 oz. Old Fashioned (1932-1978). On the right is the early version, with straight sides and no ridge, $18-25; on the left is the later version, with slanted sides and a ridge at the base, $18-25.

160, 6 oz. Juice Tumbler (1932-1979). Later version with ridge on left, $12-15; early version with straight sides and no ridge on right, $12-15.

1600 Stem Line: 1947-1968

Due to its shorter production life, the 1600 series of stems shown next is not seen on the market as frequently as the 1602 series. Most of the 1602 series stems have a flat bottom on the bowl part of the stemware, while the 1600 stems have a more graceful rounded bottom of the bowl. The 1600 series includes limited items in Cranberry Stain and Evergreen, which will be shown in the color section.

1600 series, 6 oz. Juice Tumbler, $30-35; 12 oz. Footed Ice Tea, $25-30; 10 oz. Goblet, $25-30. Also included in the photograph is the 160, 14 oz. Goblet (AKA Hoffman House Goblet) for a comparison of size to the 1600, 10 oz. Goblet.

Left: 160, 14 oz. Old Fashioned, 1/4" base ridge (1954-1978), $25-35; Center: 160, 7 oz. Old Fashioned with base ridge (1967-1978), $18-25; Right: 160, 2 1/2 oz. Whiskey (1932-1964), $20-22.

1600, 3 oz. Wine, $35-40; 3 1/2 oz. Cocktail, $30-35; 6 oz. Sherbet, $25-30.

1601 Tumbler Line: 1951

1601, 6 oz. Juice Tumbler; 9 oz. Water Tumbler; 12 oz. Ice Tea Tumbler, $35-45 each. These barrel shape tumblers are very difficult to find due to their short production time of one year, 1951.

1602 Series: 1942-1983

Remember that the stems from 1932 up to and including 1942 had a wafer stem. Introduced in 1942 was the 1602 Series of stemware, which had what has come to be called the fancy stem. These two groups overlapped in the 1942 catalog. The fancy stem consists of a ball shape with small diamond points. It is also referred to as the strawberry or mitre stem. The 1602 line is a little heavier than the 160 wafer line.

1602, 12 oz. Footed Ice Tea Tumbler (1942-1983), $15-20; 10 oz. Footed Tumbler (1946-1973), $12-15; 4 oz. Oyster or Fruit Cocktail (1942-1971), $15-20; 6 oz. Footed Juice Tumbler (1942-1976), $12-15.

1602, 11 oz. Goblet (1942-1983), $12-15; 9 oz. Luncheon Goblet (1942-1974), $10-12; 6 oz. Tall Sherbet or Saucer Champagne (1942-1979), $10-15; 6 oz. Low Sundae (1942-1983), $10-12.

1602, 5 oz. Claret or Wine (1942-1983), $12-15; 3 1/2 oz. Cocktail (1942-1973), $10-12; 3 oz. Wine (1942-1974), $12-15.

1602, 2 1/2 oz. Sherry (1951), $50-75; 1 1/2 oz. Cordial (1946-1973), $12-15; 1602, 6 oz. Parfait (1951-1974), $12-18. The cordial was used for the 1602 Cigarette Lighter, which comes in Milk Glass, Black, Ruby and Purple Slag. You might find these with the lighter mechanism missing and consider it as a colored cordial.

1602 Concave Stems: 1940-1942

The following photograph features three items that have a concave stem. These items were made 1940-1942 only. They are often overlooked because collectors do not always inspect the stems of every piece.

1602, 12 oz. Footed Ice Tea (1940-1942), $30-40; 6 oz. Footed Juice Glass (1940-1942), $30-40; 4 oz. Oyster or Fruit Cocktail (1940-1942), $30-40; note the concave stem.

3600 Blown Stem: 1951-1957

After the first edition of our book, we were questioned why we included this 3600 Series of stems. Our response was because they were called Blown Cape Cod and had the fancy stem. We have never had a second thought about including the blown stems and we think this part of the Cape Cod pattern is elegant. We have been told that the buyers of Cape Cod asked for a lighter, more elegant line of stems to go with the Cape Cod line and other fine china; blown Cape Cod was the answer. It sets a beautiful table. The 3600 line is very difficult to find but well worth the wait.

The Blown Cape Cod line was also produced with four different cut patterns that will be discussed on page 102.

3600, 11 oz. Goblet (1951-1957), $35-45; 12 oz. Ice Tea Tumbler (1951-1957), $35-45; 6 oz. Juice (1951-1957), $35-45; 6 oz. Sherbet (1951-1957), $35-45.

3600, 5 oz. Wine (1951-1957), $35-45; 4 oz. Cocktail (1951-1957), $35-45; 1 1/2 oz. Cordial (1951-1957), $*.

These next two tumblers have not been found or reported by any collectors that we have heard about. Considering the similarities between the Cape Cod line and the Candlewick line, we think that the 3611, 5 oz. Tumbler will be approximately 4" tall and the 3612, 12 oz. Tumbler will be approximately 5 3/8" tall.

3612, 12 oz. Tumbler (1953-1955), $*; 3611, 5 oz. Tumbler, $*.

Coasters, Icer Set: 1932-1982, 1953-1955

1601R, 4 1/2" Coaster (AKA 160/34 Individual Butter) (1932-1968), $10-15.

160/76 Coaster with Spoon Rest (1950-1982), $12-15. This is one of the items that does not have all the characteristics of Cape Cod. The small dots are raised and not indented.

160/85, 3" Square Coaster (1955-1968), $22-25; another Cape Cod item without all the characteristics of Cape Cod. Again, the small dots are raised, not indented as is usual.

160/78, 4" round Coaster (1947-1968), $15-20. This is another of several Cape Cod items that will escape you if you do not have prior information. Instead of the usual indented thumbprints, it has small raised bumps. When we found our first one, it was only by studying the catalogs we had that we knew we had found a piece of Cape Cod.

160/53/3, 3 pc. Icer Set (1953-1955), $85-100; #530, 5 1/2 oz. Tumbler, $25-30; #530, Sherbet or Fruit Lining, $25-30. Originally, this set consisted of these three items: 160/53 Icer Bowl, #530 Tumbler, #530 Sherbet Insert. Today, most collectors have to find and put the parts together to have a complete set. The bowl to this set has three risers on the inside to support the juice and the cocktail glass. These inserts are another example of the similarities of Candlewick and Cape Cod designs. The inserts are used in both patterns.

Cups and Saucers, Tom and Jerry Mug, Stein, Bouillon, Egg Cup

The tea cup and coffee cup use different saucers. The saucer for the coffee cup has a larger recessed seat than does the tea cup saucer. Some of the later saucers seem to be too high in the center and the cups do not sit firmly in the saucers. Collectors should watch for these irregularities.

160/200 Tom and Jerry Mug (AKA Cigarette Holder) (1947-1951), $50-65.

160/35 Tea Cup and Saucer (1937-1979), $10-12. The well on the saucer is 1 7/8" diameter. The base of the tea cup is smaller than the base of the coffee cup.

160/250 Bouillon Cup, fits a 160/37 Saucer (1947-1951), $50-55. Catalog illustrations do not show the bouillon cup with a saucer. However, ours did come with a 160/37 saucer at an early date, before there was enough information available for items to be married (i.e., combined) by sellers.

160/37 Coffee Cup and Saucer (1932-1982), $14-20. The diameter of the well on the saucer is 2 1/4" diameter.

Bowls

Always a puzzle is the subject of a marie or no marie on the bottom. A marie is that extra ridge on the bottom that measures about 1/4" and that a person can hold onto. There will be a marie if it was necessary to use a snap rod to hold the glass while the craftsman reheated the item in a furnace. In contrast, if the item had a hot metal rod stuck to the bottom to hold the piece during the reheating process, it would have then been finished by grinding and polishing. This is also discussed on page 10. Some of the bowls may be found with the marie bottom or the ground and polished bottom. Generally, the marie bottom is found on the earlier items.

160/225 Egg Cup (1947-1962), \$30-35. It is our understanding that the egg is served standing in the small end and the person being served cracks the shell and spoons the egg out of shell into the larger end of the egg cup. Egg cups are popular enough that some people only collect egg cups.

1602 Finger Bowl (1947-1974), \$12-15. Later version on left without a marie, early version on right with a marie.

160/188, 12 oz. Handled Stein (1947-1951), left, \$55-65. On the right is an example of the stein handle painted brown to have it resemble raffia. This painted handle is shown in the December 1947 issue of *House and Garden* magazine. There is an advertisement that includes a 160/188 Stein with a smooth handle, but the final design had a handle with ridges resembling raffia. The stein was also produced in Milk Glass.

1604 1/2A, 4 1/2" Finger Bowl (1932-1946), \$12-15.

Left: 160/5W, 6 3/4"-7" Flared Bowl (1932-1955), $25-30; Center: 160/1W, 4 1/2" Fruit (1604W early number) (1932-1978), $12-18; Right: 160/23B, 5 1/2" Fruit (1604 1/2B early number) (1932-1979), $12-15.

160/53X (1604 1/2X) 6" Baked Apple Bowl (1932-1978), $10-15; 160/5X, 7" Bowl, $* (shaped like Baked Apple) (1953-1955). The 7" Baked Apple is seldom seen.

Front: 160/197, 4 1/2" Lug Dessert (1947-1948), $35-45. Back left: 160/198, 5 1/2" Lug Soup (1947-1951 and again 1982), $25-35. The bowls made in 1982 are much heavier than those made originally and the tab handle is thick and a little wavy. Back right: 160/199, 6 1/2" Lug Bowl (1947-1948), $35-45.

Plates, Crescent Salad: 1932-1983

160/34, 4 1/2" Individual Butter Plate (1601R early number) (1932-1968), $10-15. Instead of the customary rayed center of the plates, the Individual Butter has dots recessed from the underside surrounded by depressed diamonds.

160/3D, 7" Plate, Salad or Sherbet (1932-1978), $12-15; (1604 1/2D early number); early plates have a marie on the underneath side.
160/5D, 8" Salad Plate (1932-1983), $12-15; early plates have a marie on the bottom. The plates changed from a marie bottom to a ground and polished bottom in the late 1940s.
160/7D, 9" Plate, Luncheon, ground and polished bottom (1947-1964), $25-30.
160/10D, 10" Dinner Plate, ground and polished (1940-1982), $45-55.
160/75D, 14" Plate (1608D early number) (1943-1979); earlier plates have narrow plain edge, ground and polished bottom, $25-40.

160/1D, 6 1/2" Bread and Butter Plate (1942-1982), $10-15.

160/12, 8" Crescent Salad Plate (1947-1949), $55-70. This interesting piece of Cape Cod can be used for so many things, e.g. serving pickles, nuts, candy, and even deviled eggs.

Serving Pieces

Serving Bowls, Spiders

Left: 160/10F, 8 3/4" Bowl (1954-1962), ground and polished, $40-50.
Center front: 160/3F, 6" Fruit Bowl (1954-1974), ground and polished, $25-30.
Center back: 160/5F, 7" Bowl (1932-1937), only one of these with a marie bottom, $35-45.
Right: 160/7F, 7 1/2" Bowl (1951-1962), ground and polished, $30-40.

160/5F, 7" Bowl (1932-1937), also shown center back in the previous photograph; another view to show the marie bottom.

160/75B, 11"-12" Bowl (1608B early number), early style has marie, later style ground and polished, (1937-1969), $30-35.

160/105, 8" Celery Dish, Bowl, or Relish (1953-1964), $40-50.

160/124, 11" Oval Vegetable (1942-1951), $80-95.

160/125, 11" Oval Partitioned Vegetable (1947-1948), $85-95.

160/131B, 12" Oval Center Bowl (1947-1955), $90-100.

160/131C, 12" Oval Crimped Bowl (1953-1964), $80-95.

160/145B, 9 1/2"-10", 2-Handled Bowl (1947-1978), $45-55; 160/62B, 7 1/2" 2-Handled Bowl (1602B early number), $25-35. The early version of the 160/145B (1942-1979) is more round; it has less slanted sides. Note that the 160/145B on the left has a ground and polished bottom. The 160/62B on right has a marie bottom. Shown in the undocumented section is an 8 1/2" 2-Handled Bowl with a marie.

160/221, 10" Vegetable Dish (1947-1951), $175-190; this is made from the 160/222 Bread Plate mold; the plain edge on the ends is wider than it is on the sides.

160/221C, 9 1/2" Crimped Bowl (1953-1962), $215-235.

160/221F, 9 1/2"-10" Fruit, Vegetable, Float Bowl (1953-1962), $75-100; 160/92F, 14"-14 1/2" Float Bowl (16010F) (1942-1951), $50-65.

1602, 11 1/4" Shallow Vegetable Bowl, Oval (1942-1943), $90-100.

1608A, 11" Salad Bowl (AKA 160/75B) (1932-1937), early style has marie (1/2" plain edge), $100-125.

16010A, 11" Salad Bowl (1 1/2" wide plain edge), marie (1932-1938), $*.

1608X, 11 1/2" Fruit Bowl (1932), $*; 1/2" plain edge, marie, wide flanged edge like 160/53X, Baked Apple (shown on left for comparison).

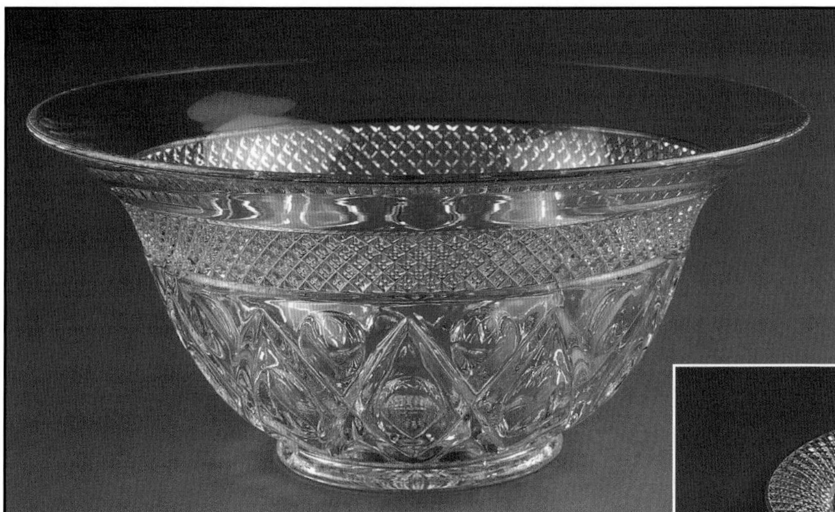

16010B, 12 1/2" Fruit Bowl (AKA Punch Bowl) (1 1/2" wide plain edge), marie (1932-1943), $55-65.

16010R, 13" Center Bowl (1 1/2" wide plain edge, top edge rolled down), marie (1932-1937), $*.

Front: 160/180, 4 1/2" Handled Spider (1947-1979), $25-35.
Back left: 160/181, 5 1/2" Handled Spider (1947-1974), $25-35; lid to the 160/144, 5" Covered Butter will not fit this spider.
Back right: 160/182, 6 1/2" Handled Spider (1947-1948), $40-45.

160/187, 6 1/2" Partitioned Handled Spider (1947-1964), $40-45.

Serving Plates: 1932-1983

The photograph below shows the 160/62D and 160/145D, 2-Handled plates. We question if there are two different sizes of the 160/62D as shown in the catalogs. Notice that the early one ceases in one year and the later one starts the next year. We have not found a two handled plate that measures close to 9 1/2". This makes us question if the early size may have actually been closer to 8 1/2" than 9 1/2" and the company then changed the size in the catalogs to be closer to the finished production size.

When a size varied slightly, Imperial would do what they called "graduate the sizes"—get into measurement that is more accurate. That there is only one size of the 160/62D is our own speculation, and we will continue to hunt for that 160/62D, 9 1/2", 2-Handled Plate!

160/75V, 13 1/2"-14" Cupped Plate (1608V early number) (1942-1971), $40-45; 160/20V, 16" Cupped Plate (1937-1970), $55-65.

160/62D, 9 1/2" 2-Handled Plate (1602D early number) (1942-1946), not shown, $*; 160/62D, 8 1/2" 2-Handled Plate (1947-1964), $30-40; 160/145D, 11 1/2" 2-Handled Plate (1947-1978), $40-50.

160/75D, 14" Regular Edge Plate (1608D early number) (1943-1979), earlier plates may have wide plain edge, $25-40; 16010D, 17" Flat Edge Plate (1932-1946), $50-55.

160/222, 12 1/2" Bread Plate, oval, wide plain ends (1947-1948), $70-85.

In a previous edition of our book, we wrote that a 12" oval plate was reported in addition to the 160/124D, 13 1/2" oval plate. Previously we had not written about "reported" items. Now we believe that the 12" oval plate that has been found is the tray to the Cape Cod Dresser Set. The interior rayed design for the oval center is wider than the interior of the 160/124D, 13 1/2" Plate. The proportions of the 12" tray fit the powder box and pair of colognes just right. The dresser tray identification number is unknown. It will be shown in the Boudoir Section.

160/124D, 13 1/2" Oval Plate (1602D early number) (1942-1951), $50-60.

Sugar and Creams: 1932-1982

Only the 160/29/30 Sugar, Cream and Tray Set was made after 1966. This would account for the availability of this set and the scarcity of the other sets. The 160/25/26 and the 160/190 are extremely difficult to find.

160/29/30 Sugar, Cream and Tray Set (1947-1970), $40-50; component parts: 160/29, 7" Tray (1947-1970), $18-20; 160/30 Sugar and Cream Set (1947-1982), $25-30.

160/25/26, 4 pc. Square Covered Sugar and Creamer and Tray Set (1947-1948), $130-150. (The lid is often missing when this set is found.) 160/26, 6 1/8" Tray (1947-1951), $30-40.

160/31 Footed Sugar and Cream Set, wafer stem (1932), $30-35; 160/31 Footed Sugar and Cream Set, fancy stem (1950-1966), $35-40. The 160/31 Sugar and Cream wafer set was redesigned to have the later style fancy stem.

160/190 Sugar and Cream Set (4 1/2" high x 3 5/8" wide, without handle and spout) (1954-1961), $*. Large is a simple description of the pair. Catalog illustrations do not show you how large this set is. What a shock when you find it.

Cruets, Condiments: 1942-1982

160/70 Oil and Vinegar with Stopper (1602 early number), $30-32. This cruet varied in design through the years: pointed stopper with pointed handle (1942-1964); pointed stopper with round handle (1969-1977); round stopper with round handle (1978-1982).

160/119, 4 oz. Cruet and Stopper, handle to mid neck (1950-1968), \$25-30; 160/119 Cruet and Stopper, handle to top of spout opening (1969-1982), \$25-30.

160/177, 4 oz. Oil and Stopper, pointed stopper (1947-1949); round stopper (1950-1955), \$30-35.

160/224, 6 oz. Condiment Bottle and Tube or Hot Sauce (1947-1955), $45-55.

160/235, 4 oz. Bitter and Tube (1947-1955), $50-55. Bitter is used in alcoholic drinks.

160/7724, 3 pc. Oil and Vinegar, $80-90; component parts: 160/177, 4 oz. Oil and Stopper, pointed stopper (1947-1949); round stopper (1950-1955); 160/242, 5 1/2" Oval Tray (1947-1951), $20-22.

160/241, 6 oz. Oil or Vinegar and Stopper, $40-45; pointed top (1947-1952) and round top (1953-1955).

160/2941, 3 pc. Oil and Vinegar Set (1947-1948), $95-110; component parts: 160/241, 6 oz. Oil or Vinegar and Stopper, 160/29, 7" Tray, $18-20.

160/2426, 3 pc. Oil and Vinegar Set (1947-1951), $110-130; component parts: 160/241, 6 oz. Oil or Vinegar and Stopper, 160/26 Rectangular Tray.

160/157, 5 pc. Condiment Set (1947-1951), $110-130; component parts: 160/55, 9 1/2" Relish Tray, plain edge; 160/70 Cruet, pointed stoppers; 160/116 Salt and Pepper.

160/157, 5 pc. Condiment Set (1951-1964), $115-130; component parts: 160/55, 9 1/2" Relish Tray, designed edge; 160/70 Cruet, round stoppers; 160/116 Salt and Pepper.

160/455, 6 3/4"-7" Square Tray (1953-1955), $170-180. The tray is listed as a 7" but ours measures 6 3/4".

160/459 Condiment Set, (1953-1955) $245-290; component parts: 160/119 Cruet with handle to middle of neck; 160/116 Salt and Pepper; 160/455, 6 3/4" Square Tray. On a 1952 memorandum, this set was sold with the 160/119 Cruets to Cuba. The set did not appear in a catalog, but it did appear in a sketch that was in the company records. Our set came with the 160/119 that had the handle to the top of spout.

We are often asked about the 160/237 Ketchup Bottle. Catalogs only showed the ketchup bottle with a wooden lid. However, more metal-capped than wooden-capped Ketchup Bottles have been found. The wooden and the metal lids are not interchangeable. The wooden screw cap has a small metal lid inside of the wooden cap. Our metal cap and wood cap bottles came from the estate of a former Imperial representative so we know that they are right although we can find no mention of the metal lid in Imperial's paper.

160/237, 14 oz. Ketchup Bottle (1947-1948) $*; wooden cap. It also comes with a chrome screw lid but they are not interchangeable. The wooden cap has a small metal threaded cap inserted in the wood.

160/252 Covered Ketchup and 160/130 2 Bead Ladle (1947-1951), $55-70. The covered ketchup is more difficult to find than the covered mustard or covered marmalade.

160/156 Covered Mustard, $35-45; 160/6 Spoon, 5 1/4" (1947-1964), $20-25.

160/5629, 3 pc. Mustard and Ketchup Set (1947-1964), $115-140; component parts: 160/156 Covered Mustard (2); 160/130, 2 Bead Ladle (2); and 160/29 Tray.

160/226, 5 oz. Horseradish Jar (1947-1951), $75-90. This stopper and the neck of the jar are both ground for sealing purposes.

The following three sets were made for only two years. However, out of the six items comprising the sets, only the 160/202, 18 oz. Gravy Bowl was made for five years. Read carefully the individual item numbers in each group and note that the sets are numbered before the parts are numbered.

Left: 160/201, 18 oz. Gravy Bowl and 8" Cupped Plate (1947-1948), $105-125. 160/202, 18 oz. Gravy Bowl (1947-1951), $50-60. 160/203, 8" Cupped Plate (1947-1948), $55-65.

Center: 160/207, 6 oz. Salad Dressing Bowl and 6" Cupped Plate (1947-1948), $100-120. 160/208, 6 oz. Salad Dressing Bowl (1947-1948), $50-60. 160/209, 6" Cupped Plate (1947-1948), $50-60.

Right: 160/204, 12 oz. Mayonnaise Bowl and 7" Cupped Plate (1947-1948), $100-120. 160/205, 12 oz. Mayonnaise Bowl (1947-1951), $50-60. 160/206, 7" Cupped Plate (1947-1948), $50-60.

Mayonnaise, Marmalades, Ladles: 1946-1979

1600J, 5" Deep Mayonnaise Bowl (AKA 160/94) (1932-1946), $40-50; note wide plain edge of bowl.

160/23, 3 pc. Mayonnaise Set (1946-1979), $35-45; component parts: 160/23B, 5 1/2" Mayonnaise Bowl; 1600D, 6 1/2" Plate; 160/165 Ladle (one bead ladle). The 160/165 one bead ladle replaced the #615 ladle for this set. Not shown is the 160/23, 2 pc. Mayonnaise Set without the spoon, $25-30.

1604 1/2B, 3 pc. Mayonnaise (1937-1943), $35-45; component parts: 1604 1/2B Mayonnaise Bowl; 1600D, 7" Mayonnaise Plate; #615 Ladle, plain.

160/52H, 3 pc. Mayonnaise Set (AKA 160/52B) (1947-1962), $50-60; component parts: 160/49H, 5" Heart Bowl; 160/52D, 7" Plate; #165 Ladle, one bead. Note that the bowl and plate both have ground and polished bottoms. Also note that the bowl and plate in this set have a wider plain edge than the mayonnaise set in the previous photograph.

160/33, 3" Individual Jelly Dish (1601W early number) (1932-1948), $12-18. This small dish has been found on typical boudoir lamps. Be watching for those lamps.

160/89/3, 3 pc. Marmalade Set (1947-1964) and #615 Spoon, $35-45. One of our sets was found with the 160/130, 2 Bead Ladle.

160/89, 4 pc. Marmalade Set (1942-1964), $47-57. Several catalogs showed the 160/6, 5 3/4" spoon in this set, which has the bowl shaped like a shell (1942). However, this spoon was made for only a short time; the #615 spoon was then put into the marmalade.

The 160/130, 4" 2 Bead Ladle is used with the 160/5629 Mustard and Ketchup Set. The beads have the characteristics of a Candlewick ladle, but this ladle is not a Candlewick spoon. The measurements of all ladles are shown with the photograph.

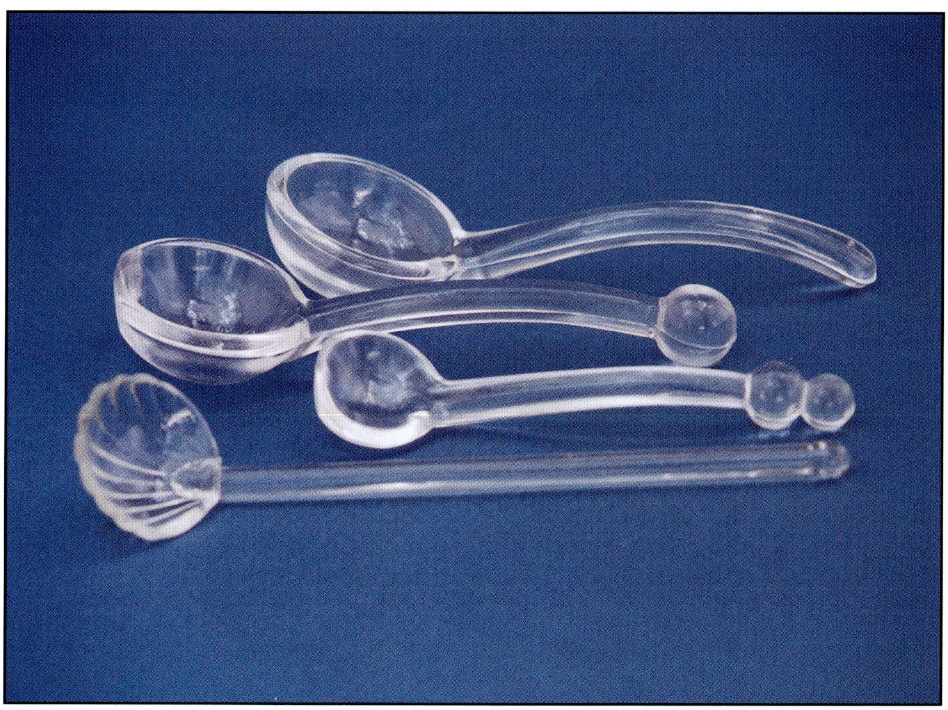

#615 Ladle, no beads, 4 1/2"-5" (ladle is also found with other Imperial sets) (1932-1946), $10-15.
160/165 Ladle, 1 Bead, 5" (1948-1970), $12-18.
160/130 Ladle, 2 Beads, 4" (1947-1970), $15-20.
160/6 Jam Spoon (1942 only), $20-25; 5 3/4" long spoon with one bead, bowl of spoon is shell shape.

Relishes: 1942-1979

1602, 11 1/4", 3 Part Oval Relish (1942-1943), $90-100. Shown here are two relishes to illustrate the variation in shapes. One has slightly flared sides and the other has straight sides.

160/55, 9 1/2" Oval Relish (160U early number), note the plain rim (1932-1951), $30-35.

160/55, 9 1/2" Oval Relish, note design on rim (1953-1979), $30-35. This is one of the easiest relishes to find.

160/56, 9 1/2" Relish, 4 partitioned and tab handles (1947-1978), $35-40.

160/102, 11" Relish, 5 partition (1946-1962), $55-70.

160/189, 10 1/2" Celery Tray (1947-1951), $55-65.

160/191, 10 1/2" Partitioned Relish, $75-95. Catalogs show this relish with a divider in the middle. However, the only relishes found to date are divided 1/3 and 2/3. The 1/3 and 2/3 relish is not shown in any catalog, but we have found a magazine advertising mat that proves that this design was advertised to the market (1947-1948). The 160/191, 10 1/2" Partitioned Relish divided 1/2 x 1/2, $*.

160/1112 Relish and Dressing Set (1947-1961), $125-150. The center jar has no design on it, but the lid has the Cape Cod design. It is interesting that the catalogs show a 160/165, 1-bead spoon with this set but the 1953 Card File has written 160/130, which is a two-bead spoon.

Butters, Salt and Peppers, Salt Spoon: 1942-1982

160/144, 5" Covered Butter (1947-1968, again 1977-1978), $35-50. No, this lid will not fit the 160/180 or 160/181.

160/161 Oblong Butter and Cover (1953-1967, again 1977-1982), $40-50. It holds a quarter pound butter stick. We have seen two bases of this set with the superimposed IG. We do not know why a few of these were marked while no other Imperial Cape Cod was marked.

During the early 1940s, Imperial put out price lists but not many catalogs. Since we generally have to rely on the pictures for much information, it is unknown exactly when the plastic lids and the metal lids were used on the salt and peppers. From what little information there is, it seems that from the early 1940s to the mid-1940s the lids were plastic and in the very late 1940s the metal lids began. These sets began with plastic lids: 160/96, 160/109, and 160/116. Metal lids were on these sets in the beginning: 160/243 and 160/251. By the early 1950s, all salt and pepper sets had metal lids.

160/61 Salt Dip (1947-1962), $20-22. The salt dip does not have all three main characteristics of the Cape Cod design; it has only the indentations and the depressed diamonds.

160/116 Footed Salt and Pepper Set (1943-1978), $25-35. This is the most common salt and pepper in the Cape Cod pattern, 18 mm lid. We know of a few sets found in a beautiful Evergreen; see page 135.

160/216, 3 pc. Salt, Pepper, Tray Set, $55-65; component parts: 160/116 Salt and Pepper, 160/184 Handled Nut (1947-1951).

160/96 Salt and Pepper Set (1602 early number) (1942-1973), 18 mm plastic lid, later sets had metal lid, $20-25.

160/213, 3 pc. Salt, Pepper, Tray Set (1947-1969), $45-55; component parts: 160/96 Salt and Pepper; 160/183 Handled Nut (1947-1969). This set in the Azalea is shown on page 135.

160/117 Salt and Pepper Shakers (1968-1982), $12-17 ea. The 160/117 Shakers use a 33 mm lid and can be found in many colors; see pages 110-111.

160/109 Square Salt and Pepper Set (1947-1951), $25-30.

160/213 and 160/216 sets shown together for a comparison of sizes.

160/219, 3 pc. Salt Dip and Pepper; $40-70; component parts: 160/109 Pepper, $15-18; 1600 Salt Spoon, $15-20; 160/211 Tray with Fleur-de-lis Handle (1947-1951), $15-25. The 4 7/8" tray is undecorated crystal with a Fleur-de-lis handle. There is a divider to hold the pepper shaker in place.

1600 Salt Spoon, 3 3/8" long (1953-1958), $15-20. The bowl of the spoon has lines in it and the handle end is shaped like a fleur-de-lis. These are seldom a perfect design so collectors must consider that when buying a salt spoon. The dates on the set and the spoon would indicate that evidently the spoon was not with the set in the beginning.

160/243 Footed Salt and Pepper Set, tall and footed (1947-1964), $40-50. The 160/243 Salt and Pepper may be found with brass as well as silver lids; they were special order with brass lids for S and P Sbanvaro Wholesale, 1970.

160/247 Footed Salt and Pepper Set (1947-1948), $45-50. This set is difficult to find.

160/251 Individual Salt and Pepper Set, small and round, 13 mm lid (1947-1982), $20-25.

The 160/236 Pepper Mill will be found with two different markings on the metal. One is the George Thompson Corporation, Los Angeles, Patent Applied For and the other is the Olde Thompson Monterey Park, California. The one with the Patent Applied For would be the earlier of the two.

In addition to the 160/2368, Salt, Pepper and Tray Set in crystal, company records note that the 160/236 Pepper Mill housing in Rubigold or Peacock color was offered to Leeds Engineering Company in 1970-1971. If you find that pepper mill, we are sure there will be much shouting.

160/2368 Salt, Pepper and Tray Set (1947-1948), $65-80; overall height 3 1/2"; component parts: 160/236 Pepper Mill with Polished Chrome Grinder, $25-35; 160/238 Salt Shaker, $20-25; 160/242, 5 1/2" Tray $20-22.

Trays, Buffet Sets: 1942-1962

On the left is the 160/149D, 8" Center Handled Tray (1953-1962), $115-130; this one was even more difficult to find than the 160/68D Pastry Tray on the right (1953-1964), $110-125 . The pastry tray was slow in finding its way to us. It seems odd that we found several colored pastry trays long before a fellow collector shared his second crystal pastry tray with us. It was a very special treat.

160/2701, 2-Tier Tid Bit Set, flat plates, wooden handle, $*. Here is another elusive piece. The wooden handle, flat plate (1943) example is rare in Candlewick but is even rarer in Cape Cod.

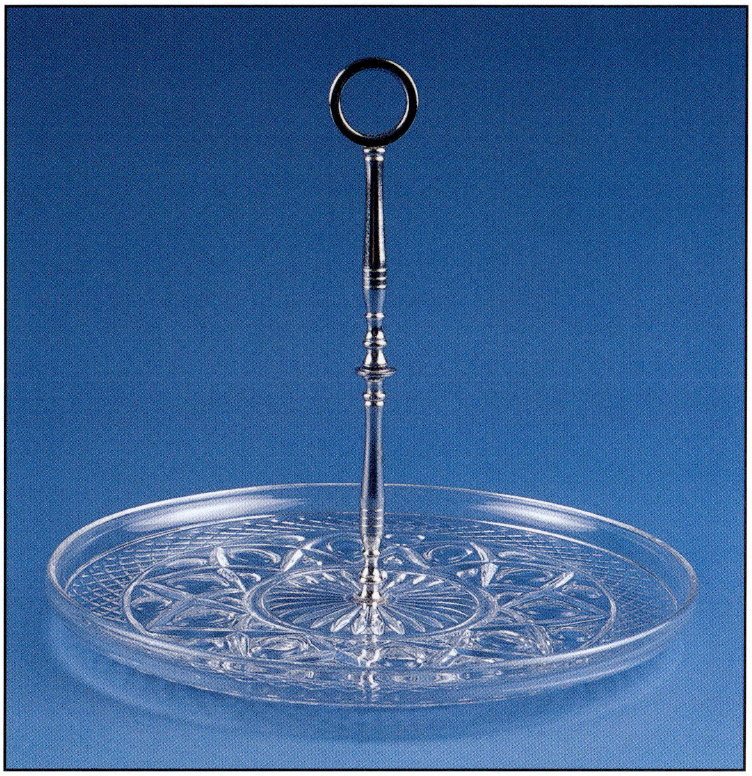

160/2701, 2-Tier Tid Bit Set, cupped plates, metal handle (1953-1955), $*. The 2-Tier Tid Bit with cupped plates is rare in Cape Cod. Neither the Cape Cod cupped plate nor the flat plate 2-Tier Tid Bid seems to have survived the years. We can only show you one-half of the set 160/2701 with metal handle.

160/94, 3 pc. Buffet Set (1947-1951), $110-130; component parts: 16010V, 16" Cupped Edge Plate; 1600J, 5" Deep Mayonnaise Bowl (AKA 160/94 Deep Mayonnaise) $40-50; 160/165 Ladle.

16010V, 3 pc. Buffet Set (1932-1946), $110-130. The only difference between this set and the preceding set is the #615 plain handle ladle and the later number for the set. Both the bowl and the cupped plate have the wider plain edge on them.

16010D, 3 pc. Buffet Set; $115-140, component parts: 16010D, 17" Flat Edge Plate; 1600J, 5" Deep Mayonnaise (1932); #615 Ladle. The difference between this set and the preceding 16010V set is the flat edge plate, which is hard to find.

Cake Plates: 1932-1979

160/67D, 10 1/2" Footed Cake Stand (1947-1979), $60-70.

160/103D, 11" Cake Stand (Pattern Top) (1954-1962), $90-100. The top part of this cake stand is the same as the 160/93 Multi Server.

In our first book, *Imperial Cape Cod: Tradition to Treasure*, we had not been able to document the 160/103D Cake Stand with the patterned top. We have now determined that the plain top was changed to the patterned top in 1954. Also, note that the patterned top is the same as the top on the 160/93 Multi Server. The rim on the plain top cake stand has the thumbprint indentations and the patterned top does not have the thumbprints on the rim.

The difference between the patterned top 160/103D Cake Stand and the 160/93 Multi Server is the height of the pedestal. The multi server pedestal is 2 3/4" tall and the cake pedestal is 5 1/8" tall. Both have the ground edge on the top of the item. Only the multi server was shown by Imperial catalogs to be used in both positions; cone base up and cone base down. The 160/103D has been shown in Price Guides as the multi server; however, the 160/93 is the true multi server. The 160/93 Multi Server is shown on page 92.

160/103D, 11" Cake Stand (Plain Top) (1947-1953), $115-135. This is the most difficult to find of the cake stands.

The 160/72 Birthday Cake Plate with 72 candle openings is always of interest to glass collectors who are not even Imperial collectors. Many birthday festivities include one of the five variously designed Imperial candle plates. The five plates include the Cape Cod, Candlewick, and three Tradition plates. Candlewick is the most expensive because it is sought by a larger group of collectors. To collectors of both patterns, the Cape Cod birthday plate is the most difficult to find and is considered by most collectors as the prettiest.

The Cape Cod birthday plate has the customary Cape Cod design elements. The Tradition plates have only the diamond points and the recessed circles. The three variations of the Tradition pattern usually are lower priced and bought by all that admire the novelty of the item.

The date of the Cape Cod patterned Birthday Cake Plate is still an elusive date for us. On a factory memorandum dated May 1948 is a mention of a "new item" 160/72 Cape Cod design Birthday Cake Plate. In the 1953 card file that contains so much helpful information, an entry shows the 160/72 reinstated 1976 (to 1978). Either the 1948 or 1976 dates could be the date we have been hunting, but we still do not have definite proof of the date.

The 1930s catalog pages show a #72 Cake Plate as a general line plate in the Tradition pattern. This same plate is shown in the Cape Cod 1947 catalog and has the number 160/72. The 160/ number designates the Cape Cod line so we have chosen to include these examples here although they are the Tradition pattern. Everyone, Cape Cod collector or not, is intrigued with the birthday cake plates. This may be the only thorough documentation on these three plates.

160/72 Birthday Cake Plate, Cape Cod design, 72 candle openings, date unknown, $300-325.

160/72 Birthday Cake Plate (1932-1951), $125-135. The early 1930s plate is not footed and has recessed circles around the inside edge of the 72 candle openings. The design covering the largest area in the center is composed of diamond points in a swirl design. The inner center is a smaller (2 3/4") circle with swirl lines.

160/72 Birthday Cake Plate, Tradition pattern (1954 and again 1983), $125-135. Imperial made a 72 candle birthday cake plate for a private mail order house and was shown in its company catalog, Tapestry. It has three feet and recessed circles inside the 72-candle opening, but the diamond points in the larger center area are in straight lines and the rays in the inner circle are also straight. We do not know of any differences in the 1954 and 1983 plates.

160/72 Birthday Cake Plate, Tradition pattern, $125-135; this version has the same recessed circles inside the 72 candle opening; diamond points are in straight lines; inner circle has straight lines the same as the 1954 plate, it does not have the three feet; date is unknown.

160/40H, 6" Handled Heart, wide plain edge (1954-1962; 1977-1979), $20-30.

160/49H, 5" Heart Shaped Mint, wide plain edge (1947-1964), $20-30.

160/220, 10" Square 4-Toed Cake Server (1947-1962), $70-80. This was the first piece of unusual design Cape Cod that we found. How exciting that was!

160/51F, 6" Handled Round Mint, wide plain edge (1954-1964), $30-35.

160/51H, 6" Handled Mint, wide plain edge (1954-1964), $30-35; free form handle attaches to center inside bottom of the mint.

160/51T, 6" Handled Tray, wide plain edge (1954-1962), $25-30.

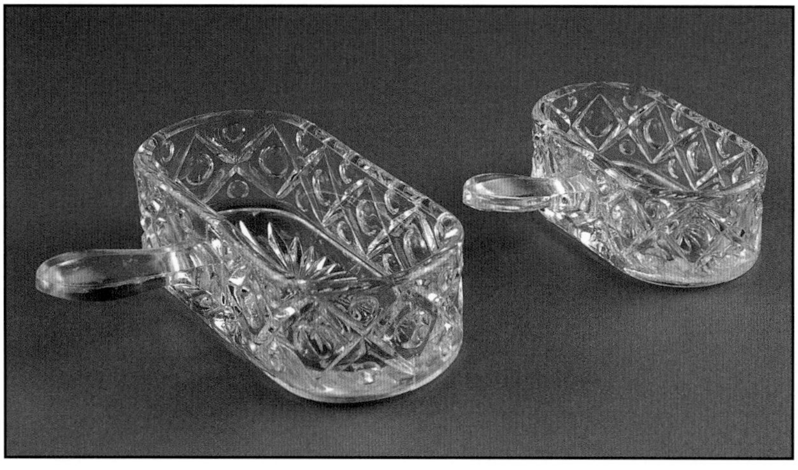

160/183, 3" Handled Nut or Mint Dish (1947-1969), $25-30; this is also the holder for the 160/213 Salt and Pepper Set; 160/184, 4" Handled Nut Dish (1947-1951), $30-35; also holder for the 160/216 Salt and Pepper Set. The 160/183 and 160/184 have only two of the three design characteristics of the Cape Cod pattern; they have the circle indentations and the surrounding indentations but there are no diamond points.

160/110, One Pound Candy Jar and Cover (1947-1962), $65-75.

160/192, 8 1/2" Partitioned Peanut and Mint Dish (1947 only), $175-195.

160/193, 3 1/2" x 4" Peanut Jar with Cover and Handle (1947-1951), $115-130. This jar is also made in milk glass under the mold number 1950/193 (1952-1953).

160/194, 4 1/2" x 5" Candy Jar with Cover and Handle (1947-1948), $130-145. In milk glass, it is the 1950/94 (1952-1955).

160/195, 6 1/4" x 6 1/2" Covered Cookie or Pretzel Jar with Handle (1947-1948), $170-200.

The handles for all three of these jars are wrapped in a beige plastic material that resembles cane. Without the lid, the 160/195 is the 160/63 Ice Bucket.

160/210, 12 oz. Handled Peanut Jar and Cover (1947-1951), $90-110. This is difficult to find because of the lid. The lid will fit any of the 160/188 Steins.

160/132, 15" Covered Pokal (1947-1951), $135-150. Finally, we were able to find the 160/132 Covered Pokal. We had wondered if this item was the 160/21 Flip Vase with the 160/40 Candy Lid. It is similar to the 160/21 and out of the same mold. However, there is one important difference. The 160/132 Jar is not flared at the top as much as the 160/21 Flip Vase. When you find a 160/132, be sure that the glass of the two parts is of the same quality and clarity and that it has not been put together. Also, be sure that the lids fit snuggly at the top of the opening without going down inside of the jar.

Pokals, Compotes, Covered Jars, Footed Bowls: 1947-1964

160/128, 11" Covered Jar (Pokal) (1947-1951), $70-85.

160/133, 10" Covered Pokal (1947-1948), $120-140.

1602, 11 1/4" Footed Oval Compote (1942-1943), $*. This is another elusive piece for collectors to hunt. It is the 160/124 Oval Vegetable Bowl on a 160/80, 5" Candleholder. However, in this instance, the bowl sides are straight and have no flare. A similar shape in the Candlewick pattern is very difficult to find, as is this one. The height of this item is 6 1/2".

160/140, 6" Covered Footed Compote (1947-1962), $55-65. The 160/48B is not the base to the 160/140. The 160/140 is straighter at the top edge.

160F, 5 1/4" Footed Compote, cupped bowl (1932-1943), $40-55; note that this has the wafer stem that was used in the early years.

160X, 5 3/4" Footed Comport, flat flange edge like the baked apple (1932-1946), $40-55. Again, note the wafer stem that was evident in the early years.

160/67F, 9" Footed Fruit Bowl (1947-1964), $70-80.

160/45, 6" Footed Comporte (1947-1962), $30-35. The fancy square design on the stem was introduced in 1947.

160/137B, 10" Footed Bowl (1947-1962), $70-85.

160/48B, 7" Footed Compote (1947-1962), $35-45. The 160/48B Compote is similar to the jar of the 160/140. On the 160/48B, the top edges are slightly flared out.

Pitchers, Water Sets, Juice Sets: 1932-1979

165, 54 oz. Ice Jug (1932-1943), $50-60; pictured in the 1930s and the 1942 catalog. The pitcher is in the Tradition pattern, but it was shown with Cape Cod in the 1930s and 1942 catalog. It was changed to the Cape Cod pattern under number 160/239 in the 1947 catalog.

160, 36 oz. Refrigerator Jug Open Lip (1932), $65-90. Due to the short production time, this pitcher is difficult to find. It has been reproduced and will be shown in the reproduction section.

160/19, 40 oz. Ice Lipped Pitcher (1947-1955), $85-95.

160/239, 60 oz. Ice Lipped Pitcher (1947-1962), $80-90.

160/24, 60 oz. Ice Lipped Pitcher (1947-1977), $85-95. This is the most available pitcher.

160/178, 40 oz. Blown Martini Pitcher (1947-1955), $225-250.

160/176, 80 oz. Blown Pitcher (1947-1964 and 1977-1979), $150-175.

160/240, 16 oz. Milk Pitcher (1947-1973), $45-55.

160/228, 9 pc. Water Set (1947-1966), $180-215; component parts: 160/24, 60 oz. Ice Lipped Pitcher; 1602, 10 oz. Footed Water Tumbler.

160/246, 7 oz. Square Pitcher, date unknown, $*. The square pitcher has a handle on the side adjacent to the spout. The square body is similar to the square 160/25 Sugar. In factory notes, there was a notation that the mold was scrapped in 1948. It is not illustrated in any catalog.

160/229, 9 pc. Footed Juice Set (1947-1955), $180-215; component parts: 160/19, 40 oz. Ice Lipped Pitcher; 1602, 6 oz. Footed Juice Tumbler.

160/230, 9 pc. Water Set (1947-1966), $180-240; component parts: 160/24, 60 oz. Ice Lipped Pitcher; 160, 10 oz. Water Tumbler.

160 Decanter and Stopper, flat, clear names on acid etched background, $125-140 each.

Decanters, Decanter Sets, Ice Bucket, Muddler: 1943-1964

160 Decanter and Stopper—Scotch, Bourbon, Rye, and Gin (1943), $125-140 each. These bottles did not appear in a catalog, but the identifying mold numbers were found on a 1943 price list. The decanters have raised names on acid etched background.

160/212, 24 oz. Square Decanter and Stopper (1946-1964), $65-75.

160/260 Decanters—Scotch, Bourbon, Rye (1955-1964), $95-110 each; names are raised words on clear background; also, flat clear names on acid etched background. These decanters are topped with the 160 Whiskey.

160/260 Decanters (1955-1964), $95-110 each; raised names on acid etched background; 160 Whiskey is top of decanter.

It is interesting that the 160/163 decanter has been produced using two different methods. The early bottles were blown in a manner that would require the bottom glass to be folded over while hot. The result would be that the decanter would have a plain bottom. The later bottles were made in such a way that the finished decanter would have a starburst design on the bottom.

160/163, 30 oz. Decanter and Stopper (1932-1964), $60-65.

160/185, 26 oz. Wine Carafe and Stopper (1947-1948), $185-200.

160/82, 16 oz. Cordial Bottle and Stopper (1947-1948), $190-210.

160/244, 26 oz. Bar Bottle and Stopper (1947-1964), $125-145.

160/256, 18 oz. Cordial Bottle and Stopper (1947-1951), $175-190.

160/2120, 7 pc. Whiskey Set (1947-1964), $185-205; component parts: 160/212, 24 oz. Square Decanter and Stopper; 160, 2 1/2 oz. Whiskey (6).

160/233, 9 pc. Cordial Set (1947-1948), $280-330; component parts: 160/82, 16 oz. Cordial Bottle; 1602, 1 1/2 oz. Cordial (8).

160/1639, 7 pc. Whiskey Set (1932-1964), $175-200; component parts: 160/163, 30 oz. Decanter and Stopper; 160, 2 1/2 oz. Whiskey (6).

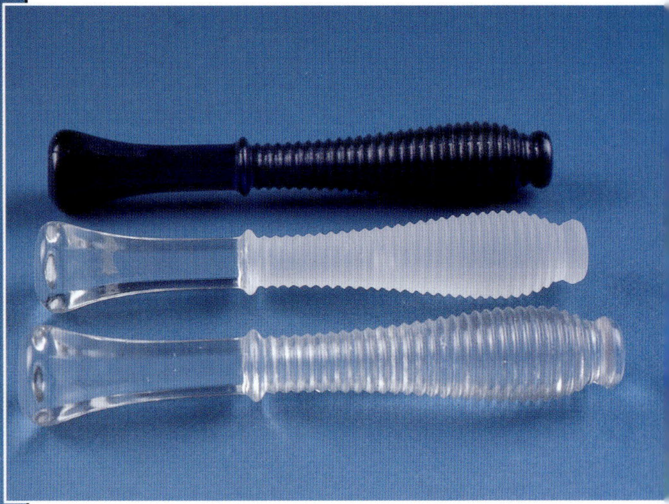

#701 Muddler (Reeded Pattern), $20-25. The Reeded muddler may be found in crystal, Satin, Ritz Blue, amber, and possibly other colors. In addition, it has been found with hand painting.

160/1630, 7 pc. Wine Set (1942-1964), $127-155; component parts: 160/163, 30 oz. Decanter and Stopper and 1602, 3 oz. Wine (6); 163, 30 oz. Decanter and Stopper and 160, 2 1/2 oz. Wine, wafer stem, not shown (1932-1943).

160/63, 6 1/2" Ice Bucket with Handle and Tongs (1947-1948), $200-225. The ice bucket is the same container as the base of the 160/195 Cookie Jar. The ice tongs are a flat metal about 3/4" wide at the center, length 6 1/2". Both the tongs and the handle are wrapped in the plastic material resembling bamboo. This, as with other items made only 1947-1948, is very hard to find

160/232, 9 pc. Footed Wine Set (1947-1948), $280-320; component parts: 160/185, 26 oz. Wine Carafe and Stopper; 1602, 3 oz. Wine (8).

Punch Bowls, Punch Sets: 1932-1970

16010, 15 pc. Punch Set (1932-1946), $225-250; bowl capacity is approximately four quarts; component parts: 16010B, 12 1/2" Punch Bowl; 16010D, 17" Flat Edge Plate; 160 Punch Cups (AKA 160/37).

160/20, 15 pc. Punch Set (1947-1970), $230-295; bowl capacity is approximately six quarts; component parts: 160/20B Bowl, six quarts, $60-75; 160/20V, 16" Cupped Plate, $55-65; 160 Punch Cup (AKA 160/37).

160/120, 14 pc. Punch Set (1947-1948), $365-440; component parts: 160/120B Punch Bowl (AKA Tom and Jerry Bowl), approximately four quarts, $250-295; and 160 Punch Cup (AKA 160/37).

160/200, 14 pc. Tom and Jerry Set (1947-1948), $800-950; component parts: 160/120B Footed Tom and Jerry Bowl, approximately four quarts, and 160/200, Tom and Jerry Mug. Because of the short production of the 160/120B Punch Bowl and the Tom and Jerry Mug, this is the most difficult punch set to find or put together.

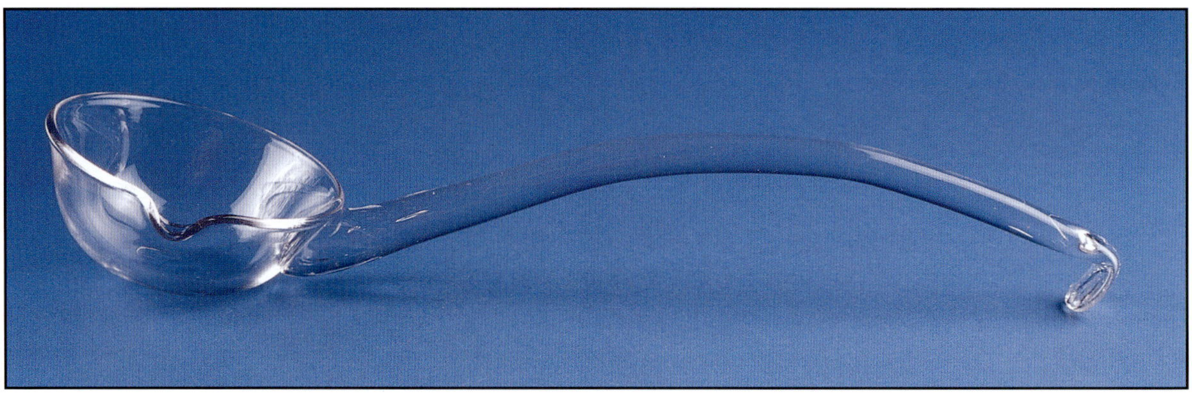

160/91 Punch Ladle (1938-1970), $30-35.

Salad Set, Console Sets, Wire Sets: 1942-1951

160/75, 4 pc. Salad Set (1608/4 early number) (1942-1969), $95-115; component parts: 160/75B, 12" Bowl; 160/75V, 14" Plate; 701 Spoon and Fork.

160/822, 3 pc. Cottage Console Set (1947-1951), $235-260; component parts: 160/221, 10" Fruit Bowl; 160/81, 4" Candleholder.

160/8075B, 3 pc. Console Set (1948 only), $80-95; component parts: 160/75B Salad Bowl; 160/80 Candleholders (1601).

160/75L (1608L) 13" Center Bowl (1941-1951) $40-55. This center bowl was not shown alone in any of our catalogs. We like to refer to this one as a gelatin mold. When you add the 160/80 Candleholders, you have the 160/8075L, 3 pc. Console Set (1608/1L) (1942-1951), $90-110; component part: 160/80, 5" Candleholder (1601).

160/8092F, 3 pc. Console Set (16010/1F) (1942-1951), $115-135; component parts: 160/92F, 14 1/2" Float Bowl (16010F), $50-65; 1601, 5" Candleholder (AKA 160/80).

160/8137, 3 pc. Console Set (1947-1951), $130-155; component parts: 160/137B, 10 1/2" Footed Bowl; 160/81, 4" Candleholder.

16010/1L, 5 pc. Console Set (1942-1946), $*; component parts: 16010L, 15" Center Bowl, $*; 1601, 5" Candleholder (160/80). Pay special attention to the wide edge on this console bowl and the rolled over effect of the bowl. This bowl was not shown alone in any catalogs.

Accessories

Candleholders, Hurricanes: 1942-1975

160/45N, 5 1/2" Flower Candleholder (1947-1951), $85-110. These two examples show the small differences in the hand finishing at the top edge—one is less curved in at the top. We have a pair of each and believe the differences are examples of handcrafting.

Imperial photograph showing the 160/45N Flower Candleholder.

160/45B, 5" Flower Candleholder (1947-1951), $75-95.

The 160/80/2 Eagle, $250-275; 160/80, 5" Candleholder (1943-1950) is shown here. It is a combination of the 160/80, 5" Single Candleholder (1601 early number) (1941-1969 and 1974-1979), $25-30; and the Imperial Eagle Candleholder. Imperial also combined its elegant eagles with other patterns. Besides this example with Cape Cod, for example, the eagle was combined with the Candlewick and Simplicity patterns. The eagles came with and without a candle socket at the back of the eagle. They also were combined with bookends, either all black or black trimmed with gold. The eagles were produced in crystal, Satin, Gold, Black, and Milk Glass. We have seen only one black eagle and have not seen a milk glass eagle so those belong in the endangered species group.

160/48B, 6" Flower Candle Centerpiece (1947-1951), $95-125.

160/81, 4" Candleholder, base is a square of undecorated glass (1947-1951), $30-35.

160/100 Twin Candleholder (1947-1962), $60-75. The glass in this candleholder has always stood out as being very special. It is one of the most elegant of the Cape Cod candleholders and is often overlooked as being the Cape Cod pattern.

160/90, 4" Aladdin Candleholder (1951 only), $120-135. This is the 160/208, 6 oz. Salad Dressing Bowl mold with a candle cup plunger used in the mold.

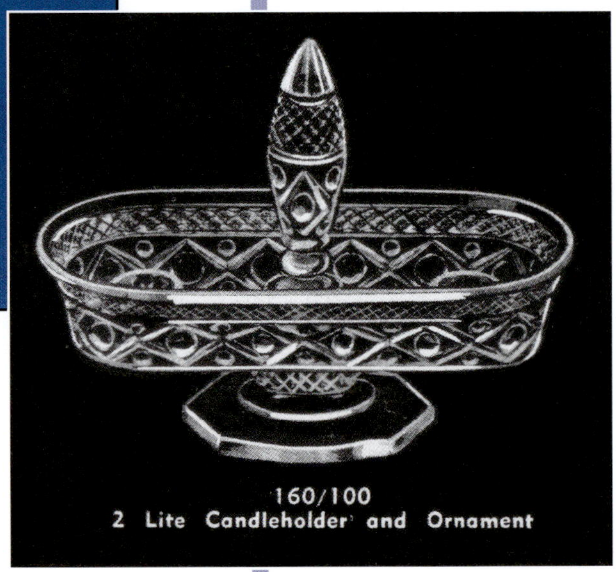

160/170, 3" Single Candleholder (1953-1962), $20-25. This candleholder was made in Verde green in 1977 for Star Exclusive; see page 130.

160/100, 2 Lite Candleholder and Ornament (1947-1948), $*. With the ornament removed, the candleholder can receive three candles. We have not heard of any collector finding the ornament. Notice that the ornament, as shown at left, has all three of the Cape Cod design characteristics.

160/175, 4 1/2" Saucer Candleholder (1604W early number) (1932-1943 and again 1953-1962), $40-45.

1604, 2 pc. Hurricane Lamp (1942-1946), $140-160. This is the saucer candleholder with an 8 1/4" shade. The same shade goes on the Candlewick 400/76 Hurricane. There is another shade that is 7 1/2" tall. The difference in these two shades is that one has a 1" longer neck at the bottom.

16880 Spider Candleholder, 4 1/2" (1974-1975), $55-75. This candleholder has a 2" diameter raised ridge in the inside of the bowl to hold a 2" candle. It was made during the time that Lenox owned Imperial Glass. Though it was made in later years, it is not easily found. Did you know it is difficult to find a 2" candle today?

Vases: 1942-1962

160/79, 2 pc. Hurricane Lamp, 9" overall height (1947-1951), $* (not shown); 160/79, 2 pc. Hurricane 12" (1953-1955 and again 1977-1980), $110-130 (shown here). The 9" hurricane presents a mystery to us. We have found several of the 12" Hurricanes but have not found one that measures 9". When studying the Imperial catalogs the proportion of the 9" and 12" hurricane illustrations look to be the same. The base looks like a 160/53X Baked Apple turned upside down. It comes in two versions: three ridges 3/8" long or small raised dots to support the shades. It may be that the different styles represent a different date of production. West Virginia Glass Company made the shade for this 12" hurricane and the shade is 10 1/2".

1603, 11 1/2" Footed Flip Vase (1942-1943), $*. This straight sided version is not easy to find in crystal; occasionally it can be found in the Ruby Flashed.

160/21, 11 1/2" Footed Flip Vase (1946-1951), $70-85.

In catalogs, there are two sizes of the 160/22 Vase. The 7 1/2" Footed Vase was made 1947-1948, $*. The vase in either size does not appear in 1949 or 1950 price lists or catalogs. It would seem that with 1 1/4" difference in size it would have to be two separate molds. An avid collector would want to be on the watch for both sizes, just in case there are two different vases. In addition, the 7 1/2" vase is the bottom of the 160/133 Covered Pokal.

160/22, 6 1/4" Footed Vase (1951-1962), $45-55, not shown is the 160/22, 7 1/2" Footed Vase (1947-1948), $*.

160/28, 8 1/2" Footed Vase (1947-1951), $45-65. The 160/28 is the bottom of the 160/128 Covered Jar and has less flare than the covered jar.

160/27, 6 3/4"-7" Footed Bud Vase (1947 and 1951-1955), $35-45. The earliest version dated 1947 was 7" and the later version was 6 3/4". These are catalog measurements. This vase was also made for Irving W. Rice. We doubt there are two different vases as we feel an adjustment was made in the catalog measurement.

160/87F, 8" Fan Vase (1947 only), $200-225. It is very difficult to find this fan vase. Experimental fan vases were made in 1984 using different dry chemicals. The top edges of these experimental vases were imperfect and the vase was not put back into production.

160/110B, 6 1/2" Footed Vase (1947-1948), $75-85. The same mold that was used for this footed vase was also used for the One Pound Candy Jar and Cover, 160/110. The only difference is that the vase is flared out at the top.

160/143, 8 1/2" Flip Vase (1602 early number) (1942-1955), $60-75.

160/186, 10 1/2", 2-Handled Urn Vase (1947-1948), $140-160. Here is another difficult item to find. The short production life accounts for its scarcity. It is the same mold as the 160/185 Carafe with a second handle added for the urn vase.

160/192, 10" Cylinder Vase (1947-1962), $135-150.

160/196, 2 pc. Epergne, 12" overall height (1947-1955), $180-200. The vase in this epergne is very unusual and is shown here to help you identify the item if it is separated at an estate sale or similar event. The vase for the 160/196 is likely to be overlooked if it is not in the epergne, as there are no design characteristics to help identify it.

1605N, 5" Flower Bowl (1932-1943), $*. This item is on an Imperial price list but is not pictured in any catalog or company photograph that we have. We believe that this is the 1605N Flower Bowl (AKA Ivy or Rose Bowls) because it is the shape of other Imperial Flower Bowls that have a mold number ending with the N. We now know of two of these bowls. This number was in the price list of our book, *Imperial Cape Cod: Tradition to Treasure* © 1991.

Baskets: 1947-1964

Shown here are two versions of the 160/40 Basket. The basket with the flat base is shown and listed from 1947 until 1962. When buying one of the baskets, inspect it carefully as there is often a fracture where the handle joins the body of the basket. Such a fracture could have been caused by temperature differences when the handle was applied.

The basket with the foot is the real puzzle in the basket story. We have not been able to find it illustrated in any catalog or company paper. When we found our basket, it alerted us to the fact that there was a second version of the 160/40 Basket. There is a company memorandum referencing a "new design for the 160/40 Basket," but it is not dated. It *is* documented by catalog and price list that the 160/40 Footed Basket was made in Amberglo in 1977 for Star Exclusives; see photograph on page 141.

160/40, 11" Basket, flat base (1947-1962), $*; a difficult basket to find.

160/40, 11" Basket, footed, date unknown, $145-160.

160/73/0, 11"-12" Basket (1947-1951), $200-225. This basket is made from the 160/222 Bread Plate.

160/221/0, 9" Handled Basket (1953-1964), $170-190.

Cigarette Items: 1947-1977

1602 Footed Cigarette Holder (1949-1970), $15-20. The Cigarette Holder is the same as the 1602 Oyster Cocktail.

160/150, 5" Double Rest Ash Tray (1947-1957 and 1977), $20-25; 160/134/1, 4" Single Rest Ash Tray (1947-1964), $15-20.

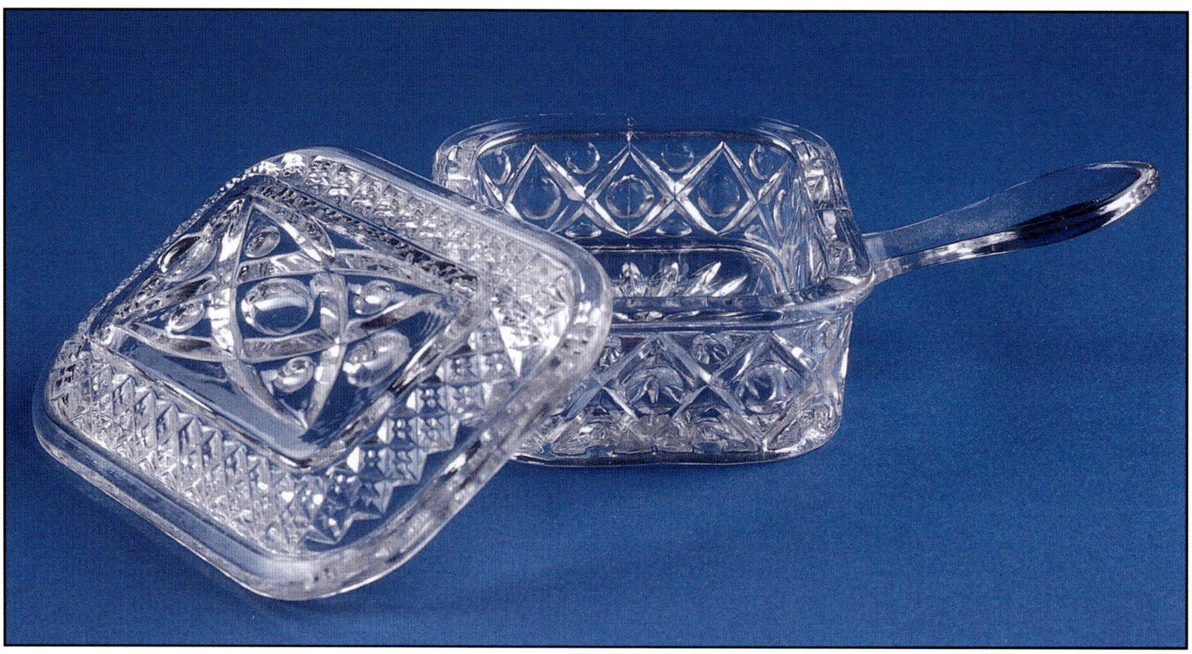

160/134 Cigarette Box and Cover (1947-1957), $35-45.

160/223, 8 1/2" Handled Cigarette Server (1947-1951), $40-55. The same item was called a Handled Server, mints and bon-bons (1955-1959).

160/200 Handled Cigarette Holder (AKA Tom and Jerry Mug) (1947-1951), $50-65.

Miscellaneous

160/123, Covered Toast, Cheese or Butter (1947-1951), $*; knob is 1" high and 1 1/2" diameter, overall cover measurements are 4" high, 5 7/8" diameter. There is no safe edge. As a set, this is very difficult to find. It is the same dome cover used in the Candlewick pattern. The catalog illustration definitely shows a flat plate. With the dome on a 160/5D, 8" Plate, the proportions look the same as the catalog picture, but we are not sure of this. It would take someone finding a complete toast set known to consist of original parts in order for collectors to know for sure what the plate is like. Considering the similarities among Imperial's other patterns, we must note that the Candlewick and Milk Glass toast plates are cupped at the edge.

160/93, 12" Multi Server (1954-1962), $80-90. The multi server has a cone base 2 3/4" tall. The base also has a more narrow plain edge on it than the 160/103 Cake Stand. In addition, the plate apron is more flared than the 160/103 Cake Stand. The multi server was designed to be used upright or upside down. It is shown here in both of its positions. There is a unique feature on the top of the multi server and the tall cake stand. The thumbprints and large diamonds are raised rather than indented as on most other pieces of Cape Cod.

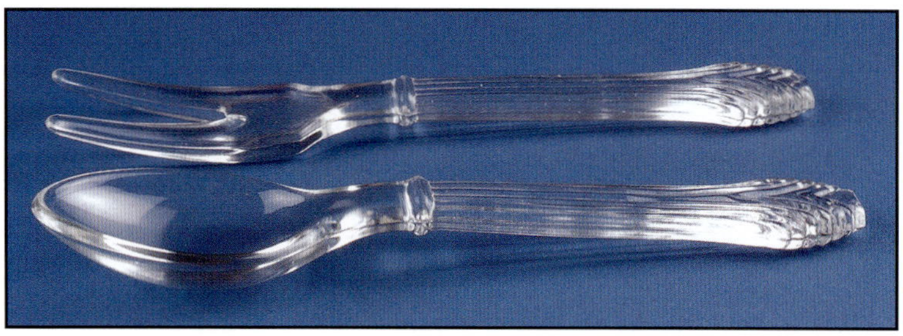

#701 Fork and Spoon (1932-1968), $25-35. This set is from the Reeded pattern and was used with several other Imperial patterns. In addition to crystal, the set may be found in Viennese Blue (light blue), light green, yellow, frosted, black, and other colors, as well as with cut designs and hand-painted.

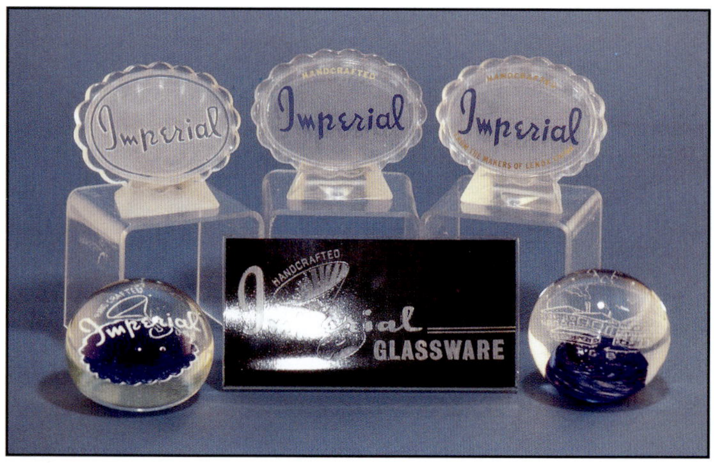

These glass signs are avidly sought by collectors, $75-200.

Imperial Glass sign; we have been told this is a gasoline sign but it certainly goes well with an Imperial Glass display, $85-100.

Part III: Colors and Miscellaneous Decorations

Cape Cod was handcrafted and pressed mostly in crystal but in a limited number of colors as well. In a 1930s era catalog, Cape Cod is listed as being made in ruby, Ritz Blue (cobalt), and amber. We have seen less of amber than ruby and Ritz Blue. The early amber is a soft amber with almost a rose glow to it. The later amber (1960s) is darker with a yellow tone rather that the rose shade.

Only the items shown will have a price guide with them. Collectors can be guided by these prices in determining similar prices.

In the 1930s era catalog, these pieces were indicated in color:

160, 8 oz. Goblet
160, 6 oz. Sherbet
160, 12 oz. Ice Tea Tumbler
160, 6 3/4" Plate
1604 1/2X [160/53X] Baked Apple

By August 1932, the list had grown to include these items in ruby, Ritz Blue, and amber.

160, 6 oz. Juice or Ginger Ale
1604W, 4 1/2" Flared Nappy
1604 1/2A, 4 1/2" Finger Bowl
1604 1/2D [160/3D], 6 3/4" Salad or Sherbet Plate
1604W [160/1W], 4 1/2" Fruit Nappy
1605D [160/5D], 8" Salad Plate
1605F [160/5F], 6 3/4"-7" Shallow Nappy
1605W [160/5W], 6 3/4" Flared Nappy
160 [160/37] Cup and Saucer
160 [160/163] Decanter
1601R [160/34], 4 1/2" Coaster

Other known pieces in ruby:

160, 7 oz. Old Fashioned
160, 2 1/2 oz. Whiskey
160B, Stem Cocktail
160, 2 1/2 oz. Wine
1608A [160/75D], 14" Plate
1608V [160/75V], 14" Cupped Plate

We have several price lists from 1937 to 1940 and no color is indicated on these lists, so it would seem that the Cape Cod ruby, Ritz Blue, and amber were only made before 1937. Please keep in mind that this information is not complete as we do find items in ruby, Ritz Blue, and amber that are not listed. Early information is very limited.

Ruby: 1932-1937

Ruby, left to right: 160 Juice Tumbler, $20-30; 160, 12 oz. Tumbler, $25-35; 1604 1/2 (160/53X) Baked Apple, $25-35; 160/3D, 7" Plate (1604 1/2D), $20-30; 160, 8 oz. Goblet, $20-25; 160/37 Cup and Saucer, $30-35. Back: 1606D (160/5D), 8" Plate, $20-30.

Ruby, left to right: 160/1W, 4 1/2" Fruit, $30-40; 160/34, 4 1/2" Individual Butter, $15-25; 160B Stem Cocktail, $30-40; 160, 2 1/2 oz. Whiskey, $25-35; 160, 7 oz. Old Fashioned, $50-60; 1604A, 4 1/2" Finger Bowl, $30-35.

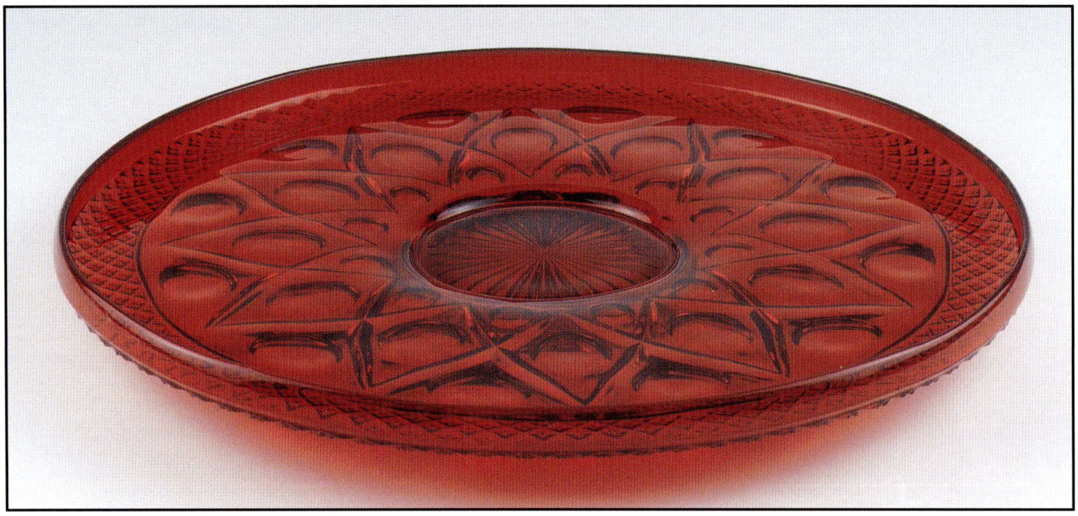

1608V, 13 1/2-14" Cupped Plate (AKA 160/75V), ruby, note the 1/2" plain edge, $100-115.

1608/4, 4 pc. Salad Set (AKA 160/75B), $275-325; ruby with crystal #701 Spoon and Fork (Imperial's Reeded pattern); component parts: 1608B (160/75) 12" Bowl, $150-200; #701 Spoon and Fork, $25-30; 160/75V Cupped Plate, $100-120.

160/1630, 7 pc. Wine Set, ruby, 1932-43, $330-350; component parts: 160/163 Decanter, $150-165; 160 Wine, early style with wafer stem, $30-35.

In our previous books, we made an assumption we have lived to regret: "Several 160/163 Decanters in ruby and Ritz Blue have been found. We have seen or inquired about approximately twenty ruby or Ritz Blue decanters and all have had clear stoppers and never have we heard of or seen matching stoppers for these decanters. Other companies in the 1930s used clear stoppers in colored decanters so that seemed to be the trend." We assumed this was the only way these were marketed. Wrong! Think of the delight of three collectors when they saw our expressions as we gazed upon their newly acquired ALL Ruby Decanter. That is the only ruby stopper we have seen and still we have not seen a Ritz Blue stopper.

160/163, 30 oz. Decanter with ruby Stopper, $*.

160/92F Center or Float Bowl, 15" (1 1/2" plain edge), $185-225; this bowl is not on the ruby list that we have, but we do think it is a general production item.

Ritz Blue: 1932-1937

Ritz Blue, left to right: 160 Juice Tumbler, $30-35; 160, 12 oz. Tumbler, $35-45; 160/5D, 8" Plate, $30-35; 160, 8 oz. Goblet, $30-35; 160/37 Cup and Saucer, $45-50. Center front: 160/53X Baked Apple, $35-45; on 160/3D, 7" Plate, $30-40.

Ritz Blue, left to right: 160 Low Sherbet, $25-30; 160, 2 1/2 oz. Whiskey, $35-40; 1604 1/2, 4 1/2" Finger Bowl, $30-35. Back: 160/1W, 4 1/2" Fruit, $40-50.

Ritz Blue 160/163, 30 oz. Decanter, $200-225; 160, 2 1/2 oz. Wine, $35-45.

Amber: 1932-1937

Cape Cod in early amber is not often found and therefore is difficult to price. However, since not many collectors seem to want amber it does not command the same prices as the ruby and Ritz Blue. As a collector, be sure to take a second look at the early amber because it is soft and attractive.

Amber, left to right; 160, 8 oz. Goblet, $20-25; 160, Sherbet, $20-25; 160, 12 oz. Tumbler, $25-30; back, 160/5D, 8" Plate, $20-25.

160/1606D (160/5D), 8" Plate, $20-25; 1604 1/2D (160/3D), 7" Plate, $20-25; the plate on left is the true early amber color and the one on the right possibly is just one of the few results of imperfect color.

Cranberry Stain, Ruby Flashed: 1949-1950, Other Dates Unknown

Shown in the December 1949 issue of *House and Garden* is the Cranberry Stain Cape Cod. It is listed on a January 1, 1950 price guide as Decoration #203. These eight pieces were documented: 1600 series, 10 oz. Goblet, 6 oz. Sherbet, 3 oz. Wine, 3 1/2 oz. Cocktail, 12 oz. Footed Ice Tea, 6 oz. Juice Tumbler, 160/1D, 6 1/2" Plate; 160/5D, 8" Salad Plate. The Cranberry decoration was discontinued in January 1950 and this short production accounts for the scarcity of this color decoration. We have one sales promotional pamphlet that shows this line of Cape Cod with Cranberry Stain under the trade name of Monticello.

Often the question is asked, "what is the difference between Cranberry Stain and Ruby Flashed?" The Cranberry Stain items are best described as lighter than Ruby Flashed items. Although we have noted "decorator unknown" for many of the photographs, the items could have been done by Imperial Glass Company. "Decorator unknown" simply means we cannot prove who the decorators were so we will leave it as unknown.

We were able to buy a set of the Cranberry Stain that was made for an Imperial board member. It includes six pieces that were not listed in the general line. Those pieces were the 160/10D, 10" Dinner Plate, 160/35 Tea Cup and Saucer, 160/37 Punch Cup, 160/20 Punch Bowl and 160/20V, 16" Cupped Plate.

160/20, 15 pc. Punch Set, Cranberry Stain, $*; component parts: 160/20, 6 quart Bowl; 160/20V, 16" Cupped Plate; and 160/37 Cups. This set was made especially for a member of the Imperial Board of Directors, decorated by Imperial.

Advertisement, December 1949.

1602 Oyster or Fruit Cocktail, $25-35; 1602, 3 oz. Wine, $20-35; 1602, 12 oz. Iced Tea Tumbler, $20-30; 160/175 Saucer Candleholder (1604W), $50-55; Ruby Flashed, decorator unknown.

Left to right: 160/35 Cup and Saucer, $*; 1600, 3 oz. Wine, $40-50; 1600, 10 oz. Goblet, $40-50; 1600, 6 oz. Sherbet, $35-45; 1600, 12 oz. Footed Ice Tea $40-50. Back: 160/10D, 10" Plate, $*; 160/5D, 8" Plate, $30-40; 160/1D, 7" Plate, $25-35; Cranberry Stain, decorated by Imperial.

1602 Goblet, $20-30; Ruby Flashed in thumbprints, decorator unknown.

160, 6 oz. Juice Tumbler, $20-30; Ruby Flashed, decorator unknown.

1603, 11" Footed Flip Vase, $95-115; note the straight sides, Ruby Flashed thumbprints and diamonds, decorator unknown.

Several different versions of the Ruby Flashed 160/143, 8 1/2" Flip Vase have been found. On most, the dark ruby flashing is on the top edge and in the large diamond indentations. On some, there is a line of gold in the indentations above and below the band of diamond points.

160/143, 8 1/2" Flip Vase (1602), $95-115; Ruby Flashed in depressed diamonds, touches of gold, decorator unknown.

160/21, 11" Footed Flip Vase, $95-115; Ruby Flashed thumbprints and depressed diamonds, decorator unknown.

160/70 Cruet (1602), pointed stopper and pointed handle, $85-115; Ruby Flashed thumbprints, decorator unknown.

160/163, 30 oz. Decanter, $150-195; Ruby Flashed depressed diamonds; 1602, 3 oz. Wine, $20-30, only diamond band is flashed, decorator unknown.

160/163, 30 oz. Decanter, $150-195; Ruby Flashed thumbprints, decorator unknown.

Cuts: 1953

As shown in the 1953 Catalog, Imperial cut four different patterns on the 3600 Blown Stems as well as on a plain #2428, 8" plate to match. The cuts are Meander C950, Celeste C951, Today C952, and Sophisticate C953. One must hunt diligently to find these stems as well as the plates.

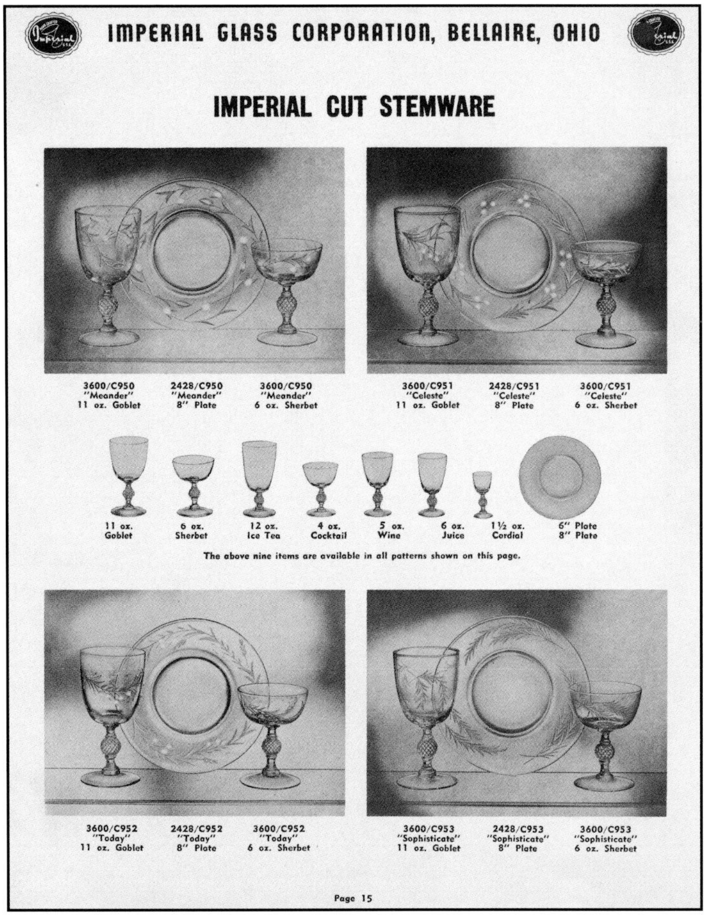

IMPERIAL GLASS CORPORATION, BELLAIRE, OHIO

IMPERIAL CUT STEMWARE

3600/C950 "Meander" 11 oz. Goblet

2428/C950 "Meander" 8" Plate

3600/C950 "Meander" 6 oz. Sherbet

3600/C951 "Celeste" 11 oz. Goblet

2428/C951 "Celeste" 8" Plate

3600/C951 "Celeste" 6 oz. Sherbet

11 oz. Goblet — 6 oz. Sherbet — 12 oz. Ice Tea — 4 oz. Cocktail — 5 oz. Wine — 6 oz. Juice — 1½ oz. Cordial — 6" Plate, 8" Plate

The above nine items are available in all patterns shown on this page.

3600/C952 "Today" 11 oz. Goblet

2428/C952 "Today" 8" Plate

3600/C952 "Today" 6 oz. Sherbet

3600/C953 "Sophisticate" 11 oz. Goblet

2428/C953 "Sophisticate" 8" Plate

3600/C953 "Sophisticate" 6 oz. Sherbet

Page 15

#2428 Plates, $*; 3600 Stems, cut $*. These plain 8" plates, #2428 from the general line of Imperial, have been cut to match the 3600 series of stems. They have ground and polished bottoms. The plates are more difficult to find than the stems, probably because they are overlooked due to the simple design of the plate, cut by Imperial, $25-35.

Imperial photograph of the 3600 Blown Stem, with cuts. Top left: Sophisticate; top right: Celeste; bottom left: Today; bottom right: Meander.

160/20D Plate; the 160/20D Plate is cataloged at 18" and this plate is 17" so it is possibly an older version. It has a gray cut (unpolished), $*; decorator unknown.

Evergreen: 1953-1955

Evergreen Cape Cod, prefix #52, is a beautiful emerald green. It was produced beginning May 29, 1953 and discontinued January 1, 1955. Documented in the Imperial card file were the 160, 14 oz. Goblet; 160, 16 oz. Tumbler; and 1600, 6 oz. Sherbet. As we were copying from the card file on that first trip to Imperial in 1980, we could not believe it when we saw the notation regarding this Evergreen. Since that time, we have seen several sets of the 160/116 Salt and Pepper in Evergreen though we cannot document the salt and pepper or the dates of production.

The 1953-1954 Evergreen Tumbler that we were so fortunate to acquire due to the generosity of two extra nice Cape Cod collectors in Houston, Texas may shed some light on another puzzle. To date, we have not been able to decide if we had the 16 oz. or the 14 oz. crystal tumblers, as all seem to measure 15 oz. When studying the dates of the 14 oz. and the 16 oz. you will see that when the 16 oz. stopped, the 14 oz. started. Since most large tumblers seem to be the same size and both hold 15 oz., and since the Evergreen tumbler is supposed to be 16 oz. and it holds 15 oz., it is our opinion that the 14 oz. and 16 oz. tumblers are the same.

There is another green 1602 Goblet about which we have little information. It was made in Helios Green, not doped. This meant that it was not sprayed with a special mix to be refired for a carnival effect. This green is very close to the Evergreen and it is difficult to see the difference without actually holding the two greens side by side. In 1972, the 1602, 11 oz. Goblet in Helios Green, not doped, was sold to Wheeling Park Commission, Wheeling, West Virginia.

1600, 14 oz. Goblet, Evergreen (1953-1955), $65-75; 1600, 6 oz. Sherbet, $45-55; 160, 16 oz. Tumbler, $65-75.

On the left is the 160, 14 oz. Goblet, Evergreen; on the right is the 1602, 12 oz. Goblet, Helios Green, $*, shown for comparison of green colors.

160/188, 12 oz. Stein (1950/200) (1950-1955), $60-65; glossy stein on left, doeskin stein on right, by Imperial.

1950/94 (160/194) Candy Jar with Cover and Handle (1952-1955), $65-75; 1950/193 (160/193) Jar with Cover and Handle (1952-1953), $85-95; handles are wrapped in plastic material resembling bamboo.

1602 Cigarette Lighter (1950/1602) (1962-1966) $40-45, by Imperial.

1950/94 Candy in Wrought Iron holder (AKA Twin Jar Server) (1953-1956), $100-125, by Imperial.

Cigarette Lighters: 1962-1966, Again 1977

The 1602 Cigarette Lighter was made from 1962-1966. The colors for these items are black, purple slag, ruby, and milk glass. We have seen six purple slag cordials together as a set and it does make you think that Imperial might have marketed them as cordials as well as cigarette lighters. However, we have not seen any records to that effect.

1602 Cigarette Lighters, left to right: black, milk glass, ruby, purple slag (1962-1966), $40-50; Nut Brown (1977), $40-50. The cigarette lighter in Nut Brown was for the Star Exclusive line and the rest were for Imperial's general line.

Bronze Brown: 1963

160/68D, 11" Pastry Tray, $95-125; Bronze Brown made for Imperial's general line in 1963.

160/68D, 11" Pastry Tray, $75-100; medium amber, shown for comparison in this group, undocumented color.

160/68D, 11" Pastry Tray, $75-100; light yellow, again shown here for comparison to the medium amber and the Bronze Brown, undocumented color.

Azalea (Cranberry): 1964-1972

During 1964-1972, there were seven items made in Azalea (AKA Cranberry), Antique Blue (AKA Heritage), Verde (light avocado), and amber (darker than 1930s amber). They were series 1602, 11 oz. Goblet; 6 oz. Tall Sherbet or Saucer Champagne; 6 oz. Footed Juice; 12 oz. Footed Ice Tea; 5 oz. Claret; 160/5D, 8" Salad Plate; and 1602 Finger Bowl.

Left to right: Azalea, 1602, 6 oz. Footed Juice, $20-25; 5 oz. Claret, $20-30; Finger Bowl, $20-30; 11 oz. Goblet, $20-30; 6 oz. Tall Sherbet or Saucer Champagne, $20-30; 12 oz. Footed Ice Tea, $20-30. Center back: 160/5D, 8" Plate, $20-30.

160/119 Cruet, handle to middle of neck, Azalea, 1969-1971, $45-60.

160/117 Salt and Pepper, Azalea, 1969-1971, $40-50.

Antique Blue (Heritage Blue): 1964-1972

Left to right: Antique Blue, 1602, 6 oz. Footed Juice, $20-30; 5 oz. Claret, $20-30; Finger Bowl, $20-30; 11 oz. Goblet, $20-30; 6 oz. Tall Sherbet or Saucer Champagne, $20-30. Center back: 160/5D, 8" Plate, $20-30. Not shown: 12 oz. Footed Ice Tea, $20-30.

Amber: 1964-1972; Amberglo: 1969-1973, 1975-1976

Left to right: Amber (1962-1972), 1602, 6 oz. Footed Juice, $15-25; 5 oz. Claret, $15-25; Finger Bowl, $15-25; 11 oz. Goblet, $15-25; 6 oz. Tall Sherbet or Saucer Champagne, $15-25; 12 oz. Footed Ice Tea, $15-25. Center back: 160/5D, 8" Plate, $15-20.

160/119 Cruet, handle to middle of neck, Amber (1969-1970), $30-40; Amberglo, (1969-1973), $30-40.

160/117 Salt and Pepper, Amber (1969-1971), $20-30.

Verde: 1964-1972

Left to right: Verde (1964-1972), 1602, 6 oz. Footed Juice, $15-25; 5 oz. Claret, $15-25; Finger Bowl, $15-25; 11 oz. Goblet, $15-25; 6 oz. Tall Sherbet or Saucer Champagne, $15-25; 12 oz. Footed Ice Tea, $15-25. Center back: 160/5D, 8" Plate, $15-20.

160/117 Salt and Pepper, Verde (1969-1975), $20-30.

160/119 Cruet, handle to middle neck, Verde (1969-1976), $30-40.

Sunshine Yellow: 1974-1975; Nut Brown: 1976-1977

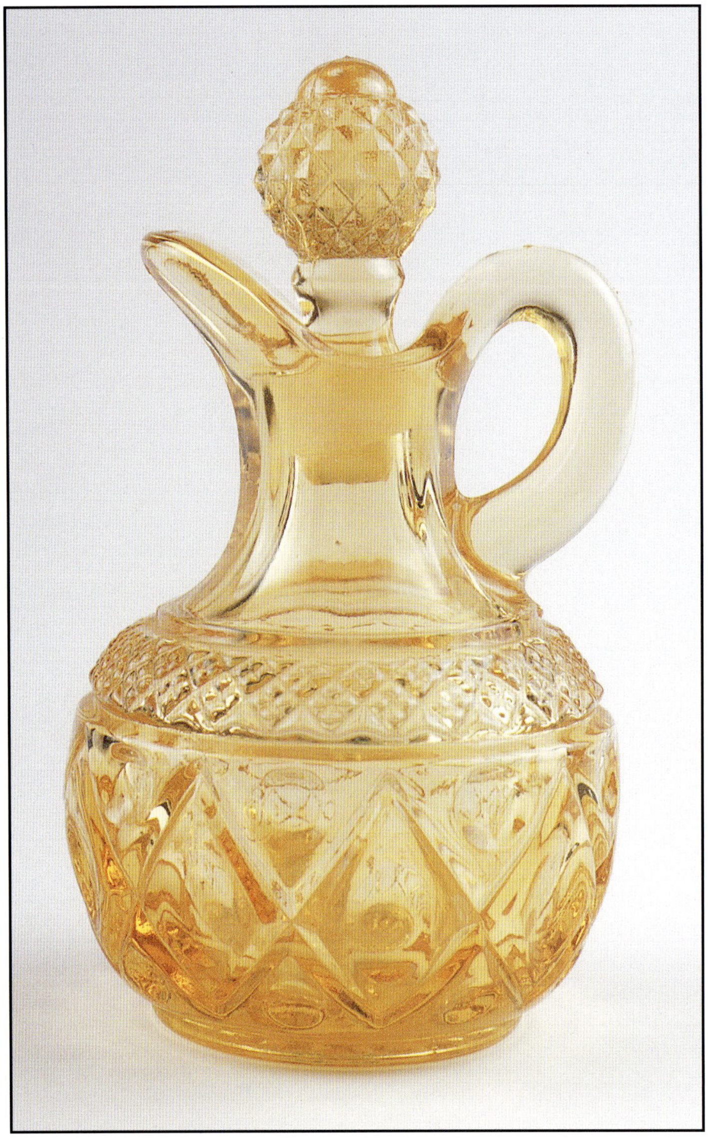

160/119 Cruet, handle to top, Sunshine Yellow (1974), $30-40.

160/117 Salt and Pepper, Sunshine Yellow (1974-1975), $20-30.

160/117 Salt and Pepper, Nut Brown (1976-1977), $20-30.

160/117 Salt and Pepper, Ultra Blue (1976-1977), $25-35.

160/117 Salt and Pepper, Fern Green (1976-1977), $20-30.

160/117 Salt and Pepper, a second look at the shakers in pairs (left to right and front to back): Sunshine Yellow, amber, Verde, Fern Green, Nut Brown, Ultra Blue; not shown is the Azalea set.

160/119 Cruets, for those collectors who like to see the items as a group (left to right and front to back): Sunshine Yellow, Verde, amber, Amberglo, Azalea.

Carnival: 1977

How is carnival glass made? In company papers we found this description: "A piece of Carnival Glass begins as a piece of brilliant, clear crystal, produced just as other Imperial crystal items are produced. What gives Carnival glass its unique, lustrous, metallic iridescence is a special mixture of chemicals that is sprayed on the crystal at high speed while the glass is still hot from the mold. The chemical spray is imbedded in the hot crystal and when permanently fired-in, creates a piece of glass that sparkles with subtle highlights of gentle iridescence." Colored glass was also the basis for carnival glass.

Many years ago, we found a Rubigold Carnival 160/70 Oil or Vinegar. It is the cruet with the round, fancy stopper and round handle. We inquired of many people about the history of this item. Someone suggested that we might contact the Levay Distributing Company. We did write for a catalogue and received it but found nothing about our oil bottle. However, we were able to find another 160/70 Cruet a few years later. This one turned out to be special because on the bottom was a needle engraved "#75 of 300 Levay 1977." All limited edition items issued before October 15, 1977 were not signed Levay, dated, or sequentially numbered. However, because of popular request all Levay Glass items sold after January 1, 1978 were to be signed, dated, and numbered.

The Viennese Blue #701 Salad Spoon and Fork is documented, but the light green and the yellow sets are not documented. Discussed in the Private Mold section of this book is a black set, with the information that it was made for T. Eaton, Company. The #701 set is also shown here with hand painting to match an Intaglio Bowl by Imperial, $75-90. The spoon and fork also may be found with a cut design.

160/70 Oil and Vinegar with Stopper (1602 early number), pointed stopper and round handle, Rubigold, $125-145; marked on the bottom with a needle: "#75-300, Levay, 1977"; Levay Glass Company.

160/25 Square Creamer, Marigold, $*; weak coloring, no information.

160/37 Cup, Helios or Peacock Carnival, $40-50; strong carnival color, no information.

160/70 Oil and Vinegar with Stopper, round stopper and round handle, Rubigold, $115-135; not signed or dated, possibly pre-1977, no information.

160/161 Butter Bottom, Rubigold, $*; no information.

1602 Tall Sherbet or Saucer Champagne, $30-45; yellow iridescence, no information.

Color Staining, Fired on Gold Trim: Dates Unknown

Another interesting undocumented color treatment is the faint color stain. We have the 160 Old Fashioned with a faint stain of pink (or light cranberry) in the indentations and light blue on the plain band around the top. We also have 1602 Oyster Cocktails with yellow flashing in the indentations in a manner similar to the yellow on some 160/5D, 8" Salad Plates. We have seen the 160/127 Bud Vase with the pink and blue stain so there seem to be more than just a few pieces of this work. Our seventeen color stained pieces were acquired at four different times and in four very different locations. There is a possibility that a company other than Imperial did this decorating and then sold its finished product. The pieces we own have a common production date of 1951-1955. These dates might someday help lead to the identity of the decorator.

160/3D, 7" Plate, blue stain in indentions, $15-20; 160 Old Fashioned, pink stain in round indentions and blue stain on edge, $15-20, after factory customer unknown.

160/5D, 8" Plate, yellow stained, $25-30; 1602 Oyster or Fruit Cocktail, yellow stained, $20-25; after factory customer unknown.

160/5D, 8" Plate, yellow stained, $25-30; 1602, 11 oz. Goblet, gold band, $30-40; 1602, Low Sherbet, gold band, $30-40; decorators unknown; 160/180, 4 1/2" Handled Spider, decorated by Lotus Glass Company, $50-60.

Included in the color group is another one that remains undocumented: the 1602 Sherbet and Goblets with a fired on gold band around the top and a gold band around the edge of the square base. Of interest is the fact that there was a pattern named Revere in the Imperial general line. In 1969, Revere was decorated with either a 1/2" fired on gold or platinum band. It may be that the Cape Cod with fired on gold was done at the same time.

We have had the opportunity to visit with a former Imperial decorator who was employed from 1935 until 1983. She shared many interesting events relating to the decorating department. For example, she said that often the company president would bring items to the decorating supervisor and ask that they be decorated in a special way for a special order or a gift. Therefore, it is possible that the gold trim on this Cape Cod was put on as a special request.

There is another special item with the gold fired on trim that needs to be mentioned. We have seen the 1601 Cologne with a gold neck. It was in mint condition and made a striking statement, $*. It was probably decorated by the same company that decorated the 1602 Sherbet and Goblet with the gold band.

Silver Overlay: Dates Unknown

Silver Overlay can best be described as a thick layer of applied silver. When the application is thin, it is better described as Silver Deposit. A large amount of silver overlay was done in Canada by customers of Imperial Glass.

There is at least one plate existing that has a complete backing of silver. We are unsure what the treatment would be called, but it does resemble a complete coating of silver. When photographed, it was difficult to tell if it was silver or just reflecting light.

160/143, 8 1/2" Flip Vase, silver overlay, $*, decorator unknown.

160/55, 3 Part Relish, silver overlay, $65-75, decorator unknown.

Metal Combinations, Wood: 1953, Other Dates Unknown

On our first visit to the Imperial Glass factory in 1980, we saw photographs of Cape Cod items in wire sets dated 1953. The sets included the 160/2701 Two Tier Tid Bit in addition to other items, which were the 160/156 (160/1) Condiment Servers; 160/70 Cruets and 160/116 Salt and Pepper Set (160/2); 160/241 Cruets (160/3); 160/56 (160/4) Relish Plate; 160/49H Heart (160/5); and 160/221C Crimped Bowl (160/6). (Numbers in parenthesis are the numbers of the complete sets.) The wire holders are brass finished metal. Just seeing these photographs made us think about researching Cape Cod. We still have not found any of those sets, but that is what is intriguing about collecting. The hunt is the fun part.

When Imperial did not decorate or put an item with wood or metal, it was likely sold to an after factory distributor. Imperial had many customers for which it produced glass, either from the customer's molds or from Imperial molds; the customer then added other decorations. If we do not know the company that combined Cape Cod with another medium, we will list it as "after factory customer unknown."

An Imperial *New Items Bulletin* dated January 1953 reads: "Cape Cod Items in Brass Finished Frames. 160/2701 will also have brass handle. Glorious and a *new* approach: Brass and crystal; Brass is strong as a home metal today and is gaining; have these sample frames only – will not order unless you sell these items here at this show!" This might give us a clue as to why these are not being found by collectors.

Imperial photograph of Cape Cod in brass finished frames, 1953, $*.

Imperial photograph of Cape Cod in brass finished frames, 1953, $*.

160/119 Cruets, Metal Holder, $50-60; after factory customer unknown.

160/94 Mayonnaise Bowl, Satin; Gold Filigree Basket, $35-45, after factory customer unknown.

160/23 Mayonnaise, Gold Filigree, 160/165 one bead spoon, $50-60; after factory customer unknown.

160/55, 3 Part Relish, Gold Filigree Holder, $50-65, after factory customer unknown.

160 Decanter and Stopper, in holder, $225-265. These decanters were not shown in any catalog but were found on a 1943 price list. Shown in the photo, with names raised on acid etched background, are the Scotch and Rye; not shown are the Bourbon and Gin; after factory customer unknown.

That next year we displayed this set at the National Imperial Glass Collectors' Society Convention. A couple from the West Coast saw the set and said that they had recently found a set like ours and sold it to Cape Cod collectors in Oregon. We compared stories and it seems that indeed there are two sets of these. We feel this indicates that the company possibly put the sets together as was suggested by the Imperial salesman. We will be eager to learn if there are more of these sets in existence. We do not think it was ever put into the general line.

160/119 Cruet set on black wood, round stopper, low round handle; 160/251 Individual Salt and Pepper, $*; probably assembled by Imperial.

In Imperial records we found a telegram from a West Coast Imperial representative. Attached to it was a sketch suggesting a condiment set made of two cruets plus salt and pepper, all in a wooden holder. Using this sketch, a former Imperial employee made us a set. It closely resembled the sketch. Years later, we found this black wood set in Colorado. It, too, resembled the sketch from the company records. We contacted the seller but the only information we could get was that they thought it was old and original. It did appear old and well used.

Lamps, Lighting Fixtures: 1930s-1940s

Lamps comprise an area that we are sure has many unanswered questions to date. In our collection, we have a pair of dresser lamps that are a combination of the 160/33 Individual Jelly and the 160/34, 4 1/2" Individual Butter. We also have two styles of table lamps using the 160/163 Decanters. Another lamp uses the 160/143 Flip Vase sitting on a heavy two-piece glass base. It is so interesting that today many new lamps have the same style as these early lamps with Imperial Glass parts. We do think that these lamps have been assembled by lamp and lighting companies.

In the past, we have found several different light fixtures using Candlewick glass parts. We have been able to attribute them to five companies. In addition, we have a Laced Edge shade plus several lamps with Washington glass parts. These, too, we have been able to attribute to specific lighting companies. However, we have found no paper documentation on the four different Cape Cod lamps that we have. Most of the lamps with Imperial parts that we have been able to identify by maker were assembled in the late 1930s and into the 1940s. That is probably the same era of the Cape Cod lamps.

We do have records showing that certain items were sold by Imperial to lighting companies. The 160/20 Punch Bowl with a 4" hole sold in 1971 to Erie Glass Manufacturing Company. The punch bowl might be in a shape to be an inverted glass globe. Sold to the same company in 1971 was a 160/163 Decanter in carnival with a 1/2" hole.

These following items went to a light company in West Hazelton, Pennsylvania, but the dates are unknown: 160/75, 14"Plate; 160/5D, 8" Plate; 160/10D 10" Plate; 160/3D, 7 " Plate. We have not found any fixtures that use these items.

We know of a floor lamp that may or may not be Imperial Cape Cod. The glass rods have the Imperial Cape Cod features, but we have no written information on this. At least an informed collector can be on the lookout for a possible floor lamp.

160/163 Decanter; table lamp, used upside down, neck cut off, $150-175; after factory customer unknown. This lamp would have to be older than the previous note about the carnival decanter. The bottom of this decanter is the plain blown bottom rather than the pressed in the mold design of later decanters.

Dresser Lamp, $*; component parts: 160/34, 4 1/2" Individual Butter Plate; 160/33 Individual Jelly; striated rod 10", beveled mirror on a brass finish base. Total height:18 1/4" from base to top of socket; after factory customer unknown. We know of two pairs of this lamp.

160/143, 8 1/2" Flip Vase; table lamp, vase on solid glass base, $175-200; after factory customer unknown.

160/163 Decanter; table lamp, upside down, neck not cut off, $150-175; after factory customer unknown. This lamp also has the early blown bottom rather than the pressed in the mold design.

The next two ceiling fixtures and other similar ones do not have the same quality and feel as other lamps shown previously, however, the quality is very good. The individual points on the band design are flat and do not have the usual four points on each small square. We have seen others like these two and one with this part serving as the base of a table lamp. We hope that the information with the next fixture will lead to future positive identification.

Hanging lamp with domed top, $95-115. We have factory records for Erie Glass Manufacturing Company, Chicago, Illinois indicating the sale of a #194 Shade without foot with a 1 5/8" hole. The dimensions are approximately the same as the 160/194 Candy Jar. The quality and design of fixture is comparable to the quality of the Candlewick general line #155 light fixture part made for the Lightolier Lighting Company. There could be a parallel comparison to these two pairs.

Ceiling fixture, another version of the previous one, $95-115. This was one of a pair, manufacturer unknown.

Perfumes, Colognes, Powder Box: Possibly 1930s-1940s

The next few photographs show several dresser related articles. Since we also collect Imperial cologne and boudoir items, it is very special to find related articles that are in the Cape Cod pattern.

1601 Dresser Set $*; component parts: Powder Box (1932-1946), $75-95; Cologne and Stoppers, $60-70; Tray (unknown number), $*. Colognes are scarce, but the powder box is even scarcer. The 12" Tray with 9" recessed oval bottom is undocumented. The colognes and box have been found with ruby flashing as well as with fired on gold decoration.

The following dresser set could be considered an undocumented set and shown in that section of the book, as the powder box is unknown. However, we feel it is more appropriate to show it here for ease of comparison with the documented set previously shown.

1601 Dresser Set, $*, Cologne, Hobnail Stopper, 1943, filigree, powder box undocumented. The stoppers are from the Hobnail line—ball shape with small hobnail bump; this combination was documented as being sold to decorators in 1943. The undocumented box in this set is smaller than the general line box and has a slightly different shape as seen in the photos; after factory customer unknown.

1601 Dresser Set, $*, Cologne, Powder Box; this is the documented cologne and box with added filigree, after factory customer unknown.

There is a May 13, 1954 factory paper that gives information showing the Guild Metal Products, Inc. buying the following:

160/96 Salt and Pepper
160/119 Cruet and Stopper
160/177, 4 oz. Oil and Stopper
160/251 Salt and Pepper, Individual and Round.

The 1954 date in the above information would indicate that the oil bottle would have a round stopper.

160/96 Salt Shaker, $60-70; adapted with pump making it a perfume, added filigree (possibly Guild Metal Products), after factory customer unknown.

Since we have the 160/177 Oil and Round Stopper shown in the next photo in gold metal filigree, we have to think that it goes with the Guild Metal Products information. This is the first information we have found that might give us a clue as to one of the many metal companies that added gold filigree to Imperial products, transforming them into boudoir accessories. Note that this 160/177 and the previous photo of the 160/96 have similar design concepts on the metal.

160/177 Oil Bottle, $95-110; round stopper, filigree, possibly Guild Metal Products, after factory customer unknown.

160/243 Tall Salt Shaker, $*; filigree at top of glass dauber, second example that we know, after factory customer unknown.

160/116 Footed Salt, atomizer, $40-50; after factory customer unknown. Others have been seen with the same obviously old bulb; it is evident that this atomizer bulb has been resting on the edge of this salt shaker for a long time. 160/116 Salts with new atomizers have been offered for sale so do not be misled by collecting fever. If it is has the original atomizer then it is desirable in a Cape Cod collection

In 1941, Imperial supplied Irving W. Rice with a 160/80 Candleholder, 5" (1601) (Irice number E-57 Mirror). This would be a very interesting find. We think this would be for a mirror stand. Also supplied to Irice was a 160/163 Decanter Stopper for a mirror base.

Irving W. Rice was one of Imperial's largest customers of private mold work. Imperial sold an enormous amount of dresser accessories to Irice but only a few in the Cape Cod design.

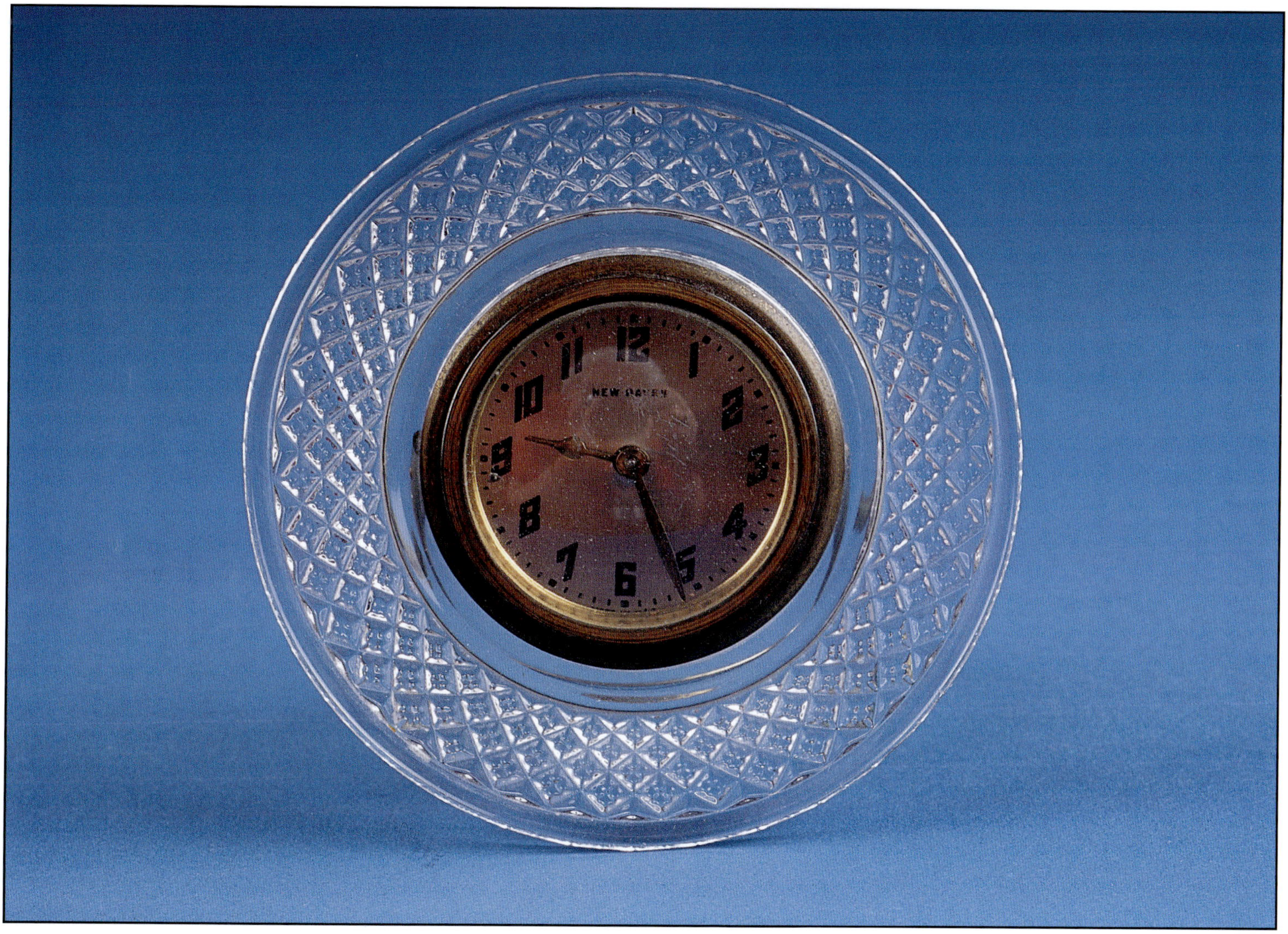

E-110 Clock using the 160/34, 4 1/2" Individual Butter Plate, $250-300; made for Irice.

Part IV: Private Mold Customers

Hotel and Restaurant

Another area of Imperial's private mold business was the hotel and restaurant trade. The only information on this comes from a 1962 and 1964 price list. Perhaps when you find an item that does not belong in the Cape Cod colored line you will find it listed in this group. We have found a 160/34, 4 1/2" Coaster in amber, heather, and Verde that we believe belongs to this hotel and restaurant group. The price list stated:

> Items listed in the Imperial Hotel and Restaurant Price List are those that are current and most popular with such customers. We have many other items from Salt Dips to Punch Bowls. Please tell us your needs. We will be glad to make items "especially" for you. We can cut, screen, hand-decorate, sandblast, acid-frost or etch. If you need a special "crest" on a Goblet, Tumbler, etc., please send a drawing of the crest and we will be glad to quote prices. We make 15 different color colors. If you are able to purchase in "sizeable" quantities, we will be glad to make ANY ITEM in ANY of our COLORS for you. [This statement may account for unusual and undocumented colors of Cape Cod items.]
>
> Colors listed are: Ruby, Green, Flask Brown, Verde, Amber, Heather, Turquoise, Charcoal Brown, Forest Green, Pink, Milk Glass, Bead Green, Blue, Gold, Charcoal, Caramel Slag, and Purple Slag. [Added as a personal annotation, the material said there were fifteen colors made, but the folder for restaurant customers named seventeen.]

Cape Cod items listed in the price list are as follows:

160, 12 oz. Tumbler (available in complete Stemware and Tableware items in Crystal only)
160, 14 oz. Goblet
1600, 10 oz. Goblet
1602, 11 oz. Goblet
1602, 9 oz. Goblet

160/1W, 4 1/2" Fruit
160/3F, 6" Nappy
160/34, 4 1/2" Plate, Amber, Heather, Verde
160/53X, 6" Baked Apple
160/55, 9 1/2" Oval Relish
160/70, 5 oz. Handled Cruet and Stopper
160/76, 3 3/8" Coaster with Spoon Rest
160/78, 4" Coaster

160/85, 3" Square Coaster
160/96, Salt and Pepper
160/105, 8" Celery Tray
160/116, Salt and Pepper
160/119, 4 oz. Handled Cruet and Stopper
160/134/1, 4" Ash Tray

160/180, 4 1/2" Handled Spider
160/181, 5 1/2" Handled Spider
160/183, 3" Handled Tray
160/213, 3 pc. Salt, Pepper and Tray Set
160/243 Footed Salt and Pepper
160/251 Salt and Pepper

160/34, 4 1/2" Individual Butter Plate (1601R), Amber, $20-30.

160/34, 4 1/2" Individual Butter Plate (1601R), Verde, $20-30; Heather, $30-40

Star Exclusives, Incorporated: 1977

In 1977, Imperial had a contract to supply Star Exclusives, Incorporated, Inc., a party plan operation located in New Orleans, Louisiana, with fifty items. These items were to be made on an exclusive basis from Imperial molds with the IG mark removed. The sample kits were made, but Star Exclusives went out of business before it got started. Of these fifty items, nine were Cape Cod made in the colors Amberglo, Verde, and Nut Brown. Amberglo was a very dark amber and is like the amber produced from 1964 to 1972.

Items in this party plan are given with their reference numbers first, followed by Cape Cod numbers:

#55420 (160/75D), 14" Plate, Verde
#55170 (160/163), Decanter, Verde
#55783 (160/170), Candleholder, Verde
#55458 (160/221/0), Basket, Verde
#55585 (160/1112), 3 pc. Relish, Verde
#55421 (1602), 5 oz. Wine, Verde
#55646 (160/40), 11" Basket, Amberglo
#55700 (160/75B), 12" Bowl, Amberglo
#55420 (160/75D), 14" Plate, Amberglo
1602 Cigarette Lighter, Nut Brown

160/75D, 14" Regular Edge Torte, Verde, $65-75; made for Star Exclusives, Incorporated.

160/163, 30 oz. Decanter, Verde, $90-110; 1602, 5 oz. Wine, Verde, $15-25; made for Star Exclusives, Incorporated.

160/170 Candleholders, Verde, $55-65; made for Star Exclusives, Incorporated.

160/221/0, 9" Handled Basket, Crimped, Verde, $150-175; made for Star Exclusives, Incorporated.

160/1112 Relish and Dressing Set; Verde with crystal insert bowl and Verde lid, $200-225; made for Star Exclusives, Incorporated.

160/75B, 12" Salad Bowl, Amberglo, slightly different shape, $75-85; 160/75D, 14" Plate, $65-75; made for Star Exclusives, Incorporated.

1602 Cigarette Lighter, $35-45, Nut Brown, made for Star Exclusives, Incorporated.

Our first Verde decanter from the Star Exclusives group had a clear stopper. Some years later, we found the Verde decanter with a Verde stopper. Now we have seen several in both combinations. Since several of each have been found, we think it is safe to think they came out of the factory with both combinations.

Miscellaneous Private Mold Customers

Producing glass for private mold customers rather than for retail market distributors was a large part of Imperial's business. This area flourished until the company was sold to Lenox and all private mold work was ceased in 1973. Only the surface of this phase of Imperial has been written about. We have only found and mentioned bits and pieces of notes that had information about the particular subject that we were researching at the time. When Imperial closed in 1984, only a small number of factory records were still there to be saved by a former employee. Through sharing of that material, we have been able to report at least some of the forgotten names and facts of this important part of Imperial's history. Remember that the following information only deals with Cape Cod items sold to outside companies.

A special order of the Azalea 160/105 Celery Tray was made for the Ocean Spray Cranberry House in 1969. We exchanged communication with Ocean Spray Cranberry, but they could not tell us exactly what the purpose of the 160/105 Celery Tray was when they were special ordered in 1969. The public relations person did tell us that the company had a gift shop that sold different types of items. She sent us a few 1960s advertisements. Some items were glass table items but none was the Imperial we were looking for. It is possible that the 160/105 Celery Tray could have been sold through the gift shop operated by Ocean Spray. That gift shop is still in operation today.

Imperial Glass Corporation had a representative in Cuba during the 1950s and early 1960s. It is interesting that the 160/459 Condiment Set was sold for resale in Cuba, and yet it is very difficult to find one in the states. Another set that is sought after but hard to find is the 1601, 6 pc. Dresser Set; that set, too, was sold for resale in Cuba. Both of these sets were sold in 1952. Please refer to pages 42 and 124 for information about these sets.

Another private mold customer was The T. Eaton, Company Limited. In 1954, Imperial made the #701 Reeded Spoon & Fork set in black for Eaton. We have only seen one of these sets and black glass collectors would like to find them.

Lipman Brothers, Toronto, Canada, bought glass blanks from Imperial to decorate and distribute as products of Lipman Brothers. Doing this is variously called "after factory decorated item." Other times it is just described as "decorated by." These items could be combined with sterling or they could have silver overlay. The following list may help you to identify products of Lipman Brothers. A factory paper dated September 1948 noted these items purchased by Lipman Brothers:

160/96 Shaker
160/109 Square Shaker
160/116 Footed Shaker
160/243 Shaker

Another private mold customer was International Silver Company, Meriden, Connecticut. Be on the watch for any marks or labels that would indicate a combination of International Silver Company and Imperial Cape Cod.

Cromwell Silver Company purchased 1602 Decanters (160/163). Several different versions of the Tantalus [holder] with decanters have been found. Knowing that Cromwell was a customer of Imperial's may lead to future identification of these items.

The following photograph shows the 160/180 Spider decorated with gold on special order in the 1990s by Lotus Glass Company, Barnesville, Ohio. We have also seen a spider with over-all bright gold decoration that was done by Lotus Glass Company, but we have no other information on these items.

160/105, 8" Celery Dish, $125-135; made in Azalea for Ocean Spray Cranberry Company, 1969, private mold customer.

160/180, 4 1/2" Spider, top edge burnished, burnished all over and outside (1950-1960), decorated by Lotus Glass Company.

160/1971, 4 1/2" Blown Salt & Pepper Mill (1971-1974), $115-135; Leeds Engineering Company, El Segundo, California. It also appeared in a magazine ad in 1969.

160/119 Cruet with Cross Stopper, $40-50; made 1968-1977 for Cathedral Arts Metal Company. The 160/119 Cruet with Cross Stopper was also made for International Silver, Company, Meriden, Connecticut, in January 1968. The 160/29, 7" Oblong Tray shown on page 34 was sold to Chaplains Aid Association, Inc, New York, 1968.

Part V: Undocumented, Whimsies, Memorabilia

Undocumented

In the company records, sketches are usually found showing items that were being considered as new items. We are going to list and give the description of three such items. If an unusual size or shape should be found, it might match one of these:

160/221B Bowl, with flange edge similar to the design of the 160/53X Baked Apple (probably 9-9 1/2").

160/271C Crimped Bowl, similar to 160/221C, 9 1/2" Crimped Bowl, but perhaps bigger or more flared.

160/271V Cupped Plate or Console Bowl; comparing the sketches, this cupped plate might be larger than the 160/75, 14" Cupped Plate.

We are not attempting to price the undocumented items, whimsies, or memorabilia because the heart rules over the head. Undocumented would be rare items and whimsies and memorabilia are usually one of a kind. The price is whatever the buyer and seller agree upon at the time of sale.

160/239, 60 oz. Ice Lipped Pitcher, amber, $*. There is a great deal of wear on the bottom of this pitcher, which might indicate that it was used for many years. The amber is not the same color as the old amber or the newer amber; undocumented in this color.

160/236 Pepper Grinder, amber, $*; 160/238 Salt, $*; Cigarette Lighter, $ *. We have seen several of the amber Salt and Pepper Grinder Sets, undocumented in this color; cigarette lighter, undocumented.

Azalea, 160, 12 oz. Tumbler; $*; 160, 6 oz. Juice Tumbler, $*. We have no information on these items; undocumented in this color.

160/96 Salt and Pepper, Azalea, $*. The 160/213 set has also been found in Azalea; undocumented in this color.

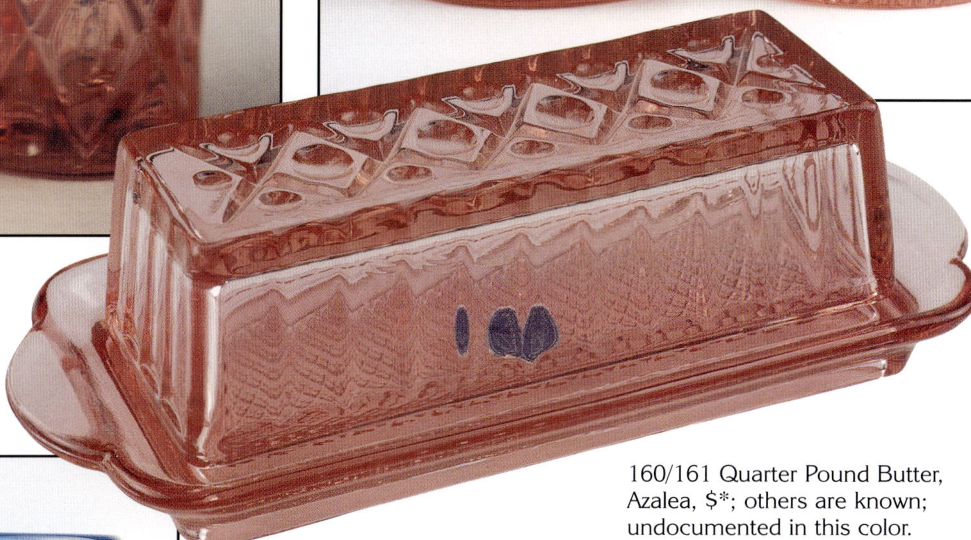

160/161 Quarter Pound Butter, Azalea, $*; others are known; undocumented in this color.

1602 Low Sherbet, Antique Blue, $*. We have no information on this sherbet, but we know that it has also been found on the West Coast; undocumented in this color.

160/116 Footed Salt and Pepper Set, Evergreen, $*; undocumented in this color.

160/72 Birthday Cake Plate, Tradition Pattern, Nut Brown, $*; undocumented in this color. The plate in this color does not fit any of the possible dates so it will have to rest without even a guess. We know that Nut Brown was made in 1977, but we have no information on these birthday cake plates being made at the time.

160/?? Compote, flared at top, undocumented; note the two wafers on the stem that are similar to the 106F and 160X Compotes. Was this a production item or simply a creation made from one of the early production compotes?

160/145, 2 pc. Cheese & Cracker, $100-110; component parts: 160/145D, 11 1/2" Handled Plate; 400/157 Cheese Compote, The compote in the center is one that is in the Candlewick line, sketch in files, undocumented.

160/75, 12" Salad Bowl; light yellow rather than just a yellow tinge to the glass; undocumented in this color.

The owner of this fantastic piece of Cape Cod is unable to determine which piece it might be. It measures 14 1/2" wide, 4" deep, has a marie bottom, inside of center seat is 3 1/2", the plain edge is 1 1/2" and the diamond band is 1". The shape is definitely undocumented.

This 2-Handled Bowl, 8 3/4" x 3 1/2" with a marie bottom, is an undocumented size. It could be just a variation of the other sizes or a completely different item that is not cataloged.

160/175 Saucer Candleholder; note that this pair is cupped rather than the usual flared style. This is either a whimsy or undocumented.

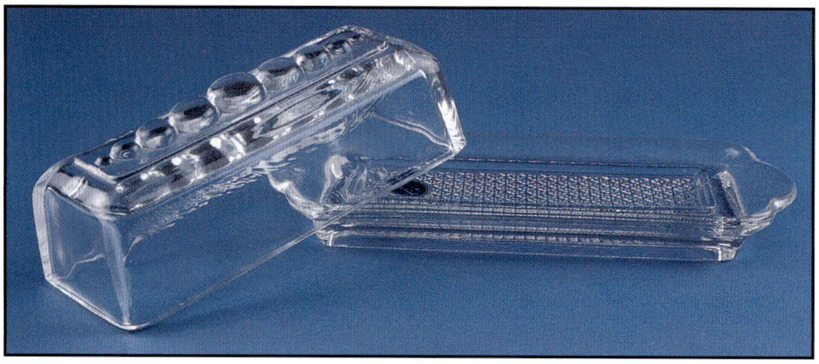

460/161 Oblong Butter and Cover. Obviously, this set has a Candlewick lid and a Cape Cod bottom. Notice that the line number is a combination of the Candlewick #400 and the Cape Cod #160. We have an actual company photograph so this set was at least considered. We bought a set like this from a consignment sale of a former employee. While it is not a pure Cape Cod set, we thought collectors would like to see it and know about it.

The drawings shown on the next page are from Imperial sketches. We have found no information on these items, and we do not know if they were ever put into the general line. Since no reference is made to them in the 1953 card file, one would have to think that if the sets were ever combined, it was before 1953. They are shown here because, documented, assembled, or not, they have a place in the Cape Cod history as possibilities.

We will begin by giving you a listing of all the items in the sketches. We are supplying the numbers we think could be the correct numbers. Those with an asterisk are the ones we do not think were made and that will be shown here.

160/??	Cordial Bottle*
160/256	18 oz. Cordial Bottle
160/176	Blown Pitcher
160/178	Blown Martini Pitcher
160/100	Twin Candleholder
160/93	Multi Server
160/56	10" Relish, 4 Part, 2 Tab Handles
160/252	Mustard (became Covered Ketchup)
160/??	Marmalade (bottom like Powder Box)*
160/250	Bouillon Cup and Saucer
160/??	Salad Set (bowl is large but shallow)
1601	Juice and Water (similar to 1601 Tumblers)
160/??	Dish, 10" or 12" Rounded Corner, one long, two smaller sections*
160/119	Cruet
160/247	Salt and Pepper
160/251	Salt and Pepper

An original Imperial photograph was found to tell us that either Imperial put this condiment set together for sale or they intended to put it into the line. The tray is made from the same mold as the milk glass 1950/85, 14" Tray. In crystal, the tray was also made for Irving W. Rice as a boudoir tray. This is a great example of the way glass companies used their molds for the various lines. Component parts: 160/70 Cruet, pointed stopper, pointed handle; 160/89 Marmalade; 160/96 Salt and Pepper; 1950/85 Tray in Crystal (AKA, M-151) for Irving W. Rice, 1942-1944, $*.

Marmalade; was it ever in production?

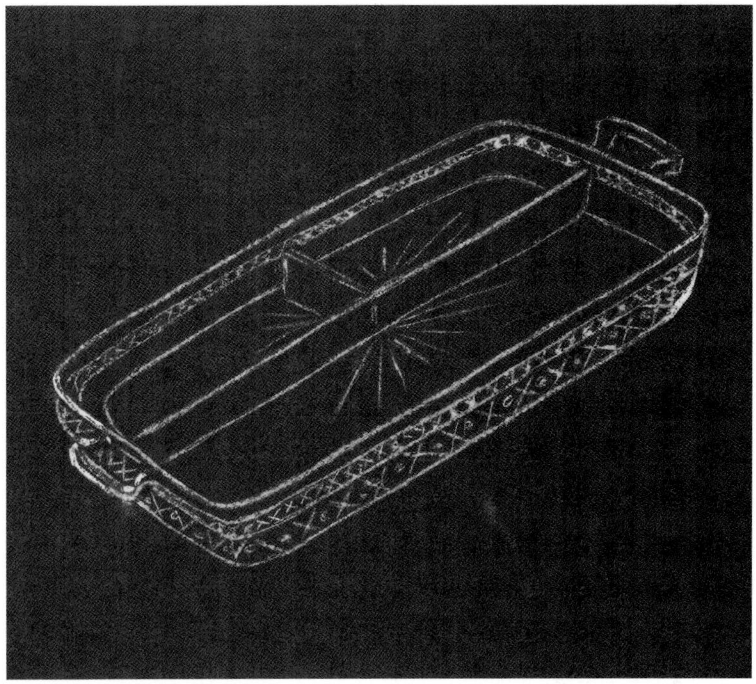

Dish, 10" or 12" Rounded Corner, one long, two smaller sections; was it ever in production?

Cordial Bottle; was it ever in production?

After the first edition of our book was published, we found two 160/161 Butters that have the familiar IG embossed on the tray. We have not discovered any information about this. Sometimes the superimposed IG mark is chiseled into the molds and other times a "slug" with the mark on it is placed in the mold. If it was done with a slug that would account for why so few are seen. If it had to be chiseled into the mold, there would probably have been many more found with the IG.

Imperial, as well as other glass companies, was constantly looking for new ideas to produce and market. The company would research an item, develop it, and then assess the desirability of the item. This was referred to as research and development. Our special 160/49H was a research and development item and a gift from the former sales manager.

160/40H, 6" Handled Heart, Cathay Finish, 1976. This was a research and development piece and was a gift from the sales manager of Imperial; as a production item, it is undocumented.

Whimsies

Whimsies are items that are made on a whim. Some have referred to them as "Lunch Box Items," meaning that the employees made them and took them home in their lunch box—the implication being that they were not supposed to be doing this. We prefer to think that when an item would not be perfect or suitable for finishing, a worker might then change it into a fanciful item. The next photograph is a perfect example of that idea. Here a footed basket was being molded. Perhaps something was not perfect about it and rather than stop the process the worker bent the basket handle over and made into a mug handle. We imagine that workers did indeed make some whimsies deliberately but when you think of how few we see in comparison to the numbers of glass articles made, the practice pales in comparison.

Because a whimsy is generally one of a kind or one of very few, we do not think that it is wise to attempt to suggest a price. Prices are strictly what a knowledgeable collector will pay a knowledgeable seller.

Is it an Ivy Ball or a whimsy? We call it an Ivy Ball; you may call it what you wish. In 1949, Imperial listed a 160, 14 oz. Goblet or Ivy. Since the catalog listed Goblet or Ivy, we think that it is the same with different names and that the Ivy looks the same as the Goblet. Imperial did make many different colored Hobnail Ivy Vases and the Cape Cod item shown is shaped identically to a Hobnail Ivy. We cannot prove the origin of the piece, but we call it an Ivy Ball.

160/40 Footed Basket, made into whimsy mug. This item probably was being made as a basket for Star Exclusive, 1977.

160, 14 oz. Ivy, whimsy.

160/100 Twin Candleholder, on crack off, whimsy.

1602 Sherbet mold, paperweight, whimsy.

160/80, 5" Candleholder, out of mold, the foot was not flattened, whimsy.

160/81, 4" Square Candleholder, on crack off, whimsy.

Three hats made from the tumblers in back: 160, 6 oz. Juice, 10 oz. Tumbler, and 14 oz. Tumbler, whimsies.

160/89 Marmalade mold, bell, whimsy.

160 Old Fashioned mold, later style, made into a hat, whimsy.

Vase flared from tumbler, whimsy.

Crimped bulbous vase, whimsy.

160/67D, 10 1/2" Footed Cake Stand, swung into a vase, whimsy.

160/180, 4 1/2" Handled Spider, flattened into a card tray, whimsy.

Vase swung from 14 oz. Magnum, whimsy.

160 Cocktail, paperweight with stem handle, leftover glass pulled out for the handle, whimsy.

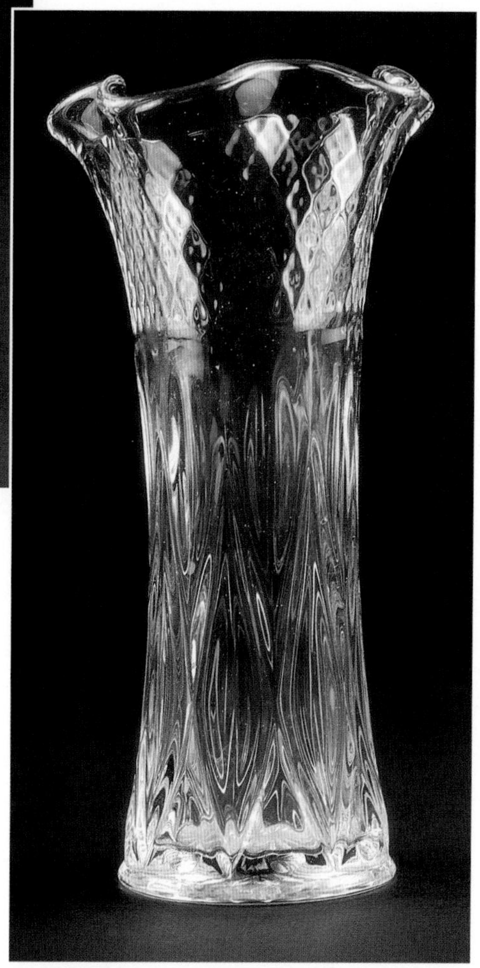

160 Tumbler, swung into vase, whimsy.

Memorabilia

We considered showing these factory models without captions and allowing you the pleasure of deciding what each piece is. However, we decided to go ahead and take a chance on making a few mistakes as some of them are unknown to us.

Models are made of an item before the design is chipped into the mold. This is done so that the craftsman may space the design for accuracy of fit. Again, these unusual items will not be priced. It is "what a knowledgeable buyer will pay a knowledgeable dealer."

Top: 160/241 Oil; 160/235 Bitter Bottle.
Bottom: 160/70 Cruet; 160/119 Cruet.

160/81 Candleholder; 160/82 Cordial Bottle.

Bowl of 160/137, 10" Footed Bowl.

160/246, 7 oz. Square Pitcher. If you look closely, you can see the drawn circle where the stick handle is to be placed. On the right is the model for the 160/25 Square Creamer.

Left to right: 1600, 10 oz. Goblet; 1600, 3 1/2 oz. Cocktail; 1600, 3 oz. Wine; 1600, 6 oz. Juice.

Now it is your turn to decide what these are. They are evidently items that were planned and had models made, but were not put into production—at least as far as we know.

Model of Cordial Bottle. The sketch of the cordial bottle on page 139 illustrates an item that we have not seen in the catalogs. It was a surprise to find that it matches the model shown. Do you suppose that it got to this stage and was dropped from production?

160/235 Bitter Bottle; wax model. After the design is chipped into the mold, wax is poured into the mold to check it for accuracy. We have often been asked, "What is bitter?" It is a condiment that is combined with liquor and other ingredients to make an Old Fashion cocktail.

Now for the best piece of memorabilia, here is another very special item. We inquired about and searched for this box for twenty-five years. We contacted Quaker Oats and they tried but did not find any information for us. Then we saw this box on an Internet auction site *after* the auction was over. We wrote the buyer to see if it was for resale. In response to our questions, the new owners answered telling us why and how they started buying Imperial Cape Cod and told us that they had our book. The box was not for resale *but* they would ship it to us as soon as they received it. We were given custody until such time as they might want it more than we did. We were overwhelmed with this generosity. Fortunately, we could later give them an item they needed, so for now both items have happy homes.

We have Imperial Company sketches that show seven items as those being made for Quaker Oats. The sketches included the five on the box plus the coffee cup and saucer. We do not know if the cup and saucer were ever actually used as premiums since they do not appear on the box.

The Mother's Oats Box pictures the Imperial Cape Cod pieces that were premiums. It was the sale of five train carloads of Cape Cod to Quaker Oats Company that saved Imperial from its first bankruptcy. Now all collectors can enjoy seeing this box—maybe for the first time. Just think, this box has survived for seventy years. It was a thrill to see the box and—through the generosity of two collectors—be able to share it for *all* collectors to see.

Mother's Oats Box. How has this box survived for seventy years? We are able to include it in the book because of very sharing collectors.

Part VI: Similarities and Reproductions

Similarities

Collectors are sometimes confused by pieces of glass named Cape Cod. There is an Early American Pressed Glass from the late 1800s called Cape Cod, but it has no resemblance to the Imperial Cape Cod. That design is one of ivy leaves on a stippled background. The only similarity between it and Imperial Cape Cod is the name. The 1800s Cape Cod is pictured in Ruth Webb Lee's *Handbook of Early American Pressed Glass Patterns*.

Other times collectors are confused by items with designs that resemble Imperial Cape Cod. Here are the most commonly mistaken items.

Tradition, another fine crystal line by Imperial Glass, is probably the most like Cape Cod of all the similarities. One distinguishing difference between Tradition and Cape Cod is that Tradition does not have the large depressed diamonds around the thumbprints. Additionally, on Cape Cod the narrow band of diamond points are on the outer edges while the Tradition pattern has the circles or thumbprints on the outer edges.

Adelaide by Pairpoint Glass Company; it is a beautiful quality of crystal with a hand cut design with all the characteristics of the Imperial pressed design. Imperial adapted their pressed design from this cut pattern.

Cape Cod is also confused with a glass called "Peanut Butter Glass," by Jeanette Glass Company. In 1991, a collector supplied information on this glass. The collector had found a "Peanut Butter Glass" advertisement in a 1957 *Better Homes and Gardens* magazine. The ad was promoting Big Top Peanut Butter by Proctor and Gamble in a sherbet, goblet, parfait, cup, saucer, and an 8" plate that all could be ordered.

McKee Glass Company produced Number 9 Line in Opal as well as crystal. Number 9 Line is very similar to Imperial Cape Cod. It has the depressed circle and the diamond point band. It is missing the large depressed diamonds around the circles. In 1951, McKee discontinued the Number 9 line. Thatcher Glass Company bought McKee in 1952 and Number 9 line was reissued in crystal. We have seen sherbets and goblets in a very pretty emerald green and the tumbler in ruby. The tumbler and sherbet were shown in milk glass in a 1958 advertisement.

Park Lane was produced by Indiana Glass Company under the Colony label and was distributed by Pitman-Dreitzer and Company, Inc.

Wexford by Anchor Hocking is often mislabeled Cape Cod. There are a great number of items produced in this pattern. It does not have the thumbprint indentions and the lower diamond shapes are raised. There is a band of small diamond points around the outer edges similar to Cape Cod. The missing thumbprints on the Wexford are the clue that the item is not Imperial Cape Cod.

Another interesting similarity is Diamond Thumbprint, made by Viking Glass Company in the 1980s. It is a reproduction of Sandwich Glass produced by the Boston and Sandwich Glass Company that was founded by Mr. Deming Jarves in Cape Cod, Massachusetts. The original Sandwich Glass was one of the most popular patterns in its time (1825-1888) and consisted simply of large diamond blocks with a sizeable indented circle in the center of each diamond. The SM symbol identifies the authentic Sandwich Glass replica made by Viking Glass Company. When we visited the Viking Company in 1982, we were given this information and the following photograph to use in our Cape Cod research.

Avon Products, Inc. made and distributed a Cape Cod pattern in ruby, but again the only similarity to Imperial Cape Cod is the name. The Avon Cape Cod is a deep red color and was made in the 1970s.

The original Diamond Thumbprint was made in crystal only. Viking issued its collection in crystal, as well as in amethyst, ruby and Colonial Blue.

While the item shown below on the right is not glass and might not confuse collectors, it is something that everyone would question and wonder about the origin. It was sent to us by a collector of other Imperial Glass. He found it and had questioned the story behind it. At the NIGCS Convention in 2002, he asked if we had any knowledge about it. Soon after, he mailed the ceramic sherbet and told us he wanted to be able to share it with Cape Cod collectors. The bowl is patterned after the Imperial 1602 Tall Sherbet, but the stem is very different. The most interesting part of this is that it has a Japan label on the bottom. We must remember that stickers can be moved. It is not good quality at all and could even be homemade. Nevertheless, it will certainly be of interest to Cape Cod collectors.

Kings Crown, Ruby Flashed; Indiana Glass Company; the only similar feature to Cape Cod is the circular indentation. Kings Crown was decorated with many different colors but ruby trim is the most common.

Shown here is an interesting piece of ceramic designed to resemble Imperial Cape Cod. It was sent to us by a non-Cape Cod collector so that other collectors could see it. The bowl part is a good facsimile of the Cape Cod bowl, but the stem and base are not representative of Imperial Cape Cod.

Reproductions

160 Refrigerator Jug and Juice Tumblers, a special premium for Tiara Exclusives distributors, reproduced in Chantelle Green by Indiana Glass, 1986.

On the left is a 160, 6 oz. Juice Tumbler in Chantelle Green by Indiana Glass Company; on the right for comparison is the 160, 6 oz. Juice Tumbler, Azalea, by Imperial.

160/161 Covered Butter. Fenton Art Glass Company made the quarter pound butter in imperial blue for Tiara Exclusives to go with their Crown pattern. (Note: The letter "I" was intentionally not capitalized by the company.) This is a dark blue and not Imperial's Ritz Blue; 1992, Fenton Art Glass Company.

L.E. Smith, Company made three items for the Tiara Party Plan Line in 1993-1995: a 160/187 Partitioned Handled Spider; 160/27 Bud Vase, which is the same mold used for Imperial's bud vase but is lacking the graceful hand shaped flared top rim; and Tiara's Cape Cod petite basket, which is probably made from the 160/1W mold, crimped and handle added. All of these items were made in Vintage Blue (light blue). One of these small baskets has also been seen in crystal.

160/187 Partitioned Handled Spider; 160/27 Bud Vase; 160/1W Cape Cod Basket; all items made for Tiara Party Plan; the small basket was not in Imperial's general line; L. E. Smith, 1993-1995.

This green pitcher and crystal pitcher are copies rather than reproductions made from an original mold. There are no rays in the bottom; copied from the 160/119 Cruet; by Kanawha Glass Co, date unknown.

We were able to buy the next bowl just before this book went to the publisher. It is the same light blue as the items made by L.E. Smith, Company for the Tiara Party Plan. However, we were able to locate the person that had been in charge of the molds for Indiana Glass Company (parent company of Tiara Party Plan). She did not know who might have had the mold to use nor for whom it might have been made. We agreed that the shape seemed to be as it came out of the mold without any hand finishing. The large light blue basket that we saw at the 2001 Convention probably started from this same mold.

Mystery Bowl, 8 1/4" diameter by 5" depth; same color as the items made by L.E. Smith, Company for the Tiara Party Plan, but we have found no information since finding the bowl a few months ago.

The 160/156 Mustard without cover shown next is very special to us. Because we had spent eighteen years at the NIGCS Convention, we decided to celebrate our 50th anniversary with our Imperial Glass friends. We had our 50th anniversary dinner at Wilson Lodge, Oglebay Park before the 1998 NIGCS convention. Since we were using Cape Cod table accessories, we wanted a nut cup that could be taken home by the guests.

What a challenge it was to find someone willing to make them for us. The first call went to Indiana Glass, present owners of Cape Cod molds. We asked if we could use a mold for the nut cup. After several telephone calls, Boyd Art Glass was happy to work with us. The mold was shipped to Boyd's and we placed our order for the color that would be in use at the time of our order. The color was a light blue slag. Since blue was a special color to Imperial it was suitable for the nut cups. We felt privileged to have Cape Cod nut cups because the first book we wrote was on Imperial Cape Cod in 1982.

There is a second chapter to this story. On our way home from the convention, as planned, we picked up the mold from Boyd's factory and returned it to Indiana Glass. Actually, they had sent two different molds so that in case one could not be used there would be a second one for back up. When we arrived at Indiana Glass, the person who had arranged for the loan of the molds asked which one we used. We pointed out the 160/156 mold and we were told that it was a gift for us. Now you cannot have a more exciting experience than that.

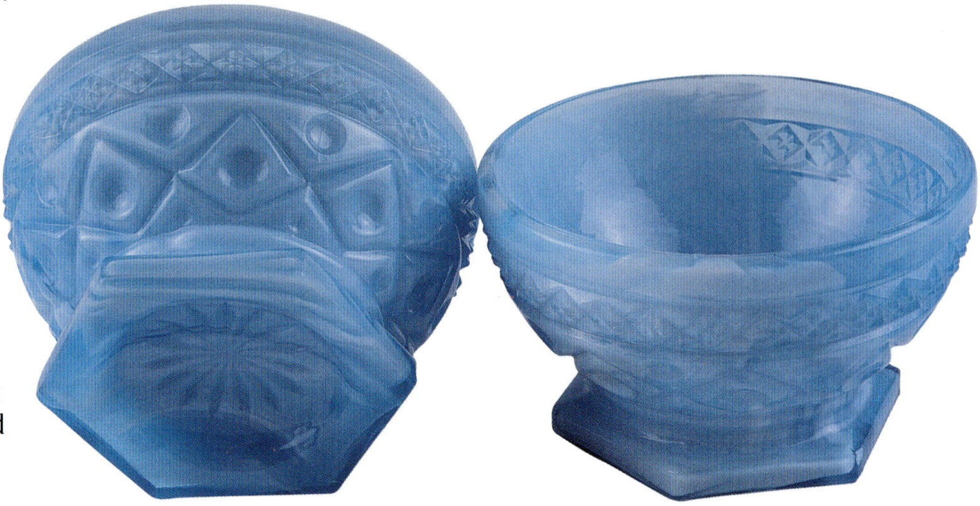

160/156 Mustard without lid, used as a nut cup for the Garrisons' 50th Wedding Anniversary celebration, 1998, marked with B & M 50th, by Boyd Art Glass Company.

This 160/156 mold was used to make a nut cup for us. The nut cup was made in light blue slag and is marked on the bottom with B & M 50th. Boyd Glass Company made them for our 50th Anniversary in 1998.

Closing Thoughts

It is difficult to arrive at an accurate count of Cape Cod pieces due to the slight variations in measurements occasionally shown from one catalog to another. We do not hope to ever have every piece of Cape Cod because there will always be the possibility of an unknown item surfacing.

Color is another area in which it would be next to impossible to say your collection is complete. An item might appear in a color that heretofore had been unknown due to lack of documentation.

Since our 1980 trip, we have made thirty-three trips to the Imperial Glass Factory area. A very sad but exciting time was spent when we were allowed to search through the basement and archives of the factory. We found many special pieces and learned a great deal about the wonderful past of a great company. We have enjoyed every minute spent visiting, reading, searching, thinking, and writing about Imperial Cape Cod and other patterns. Most of all, we treasure the people we have met and the friendships we have made. We hope our readers, whether collectors or dealers, will benefit from our efforts and pleasure. As stated in our second edition, "We have taken a risk in publishing this book. We have left ourselves open to close scrutiny, so please be gentle. Until you have undertaken a task such as this, you have no idea how perfect you are expected to be. We cannot be perfect, but we have tried to be as accurate as we can be. We hope you enjoy this book as much as we have enjoyed the research and the compiling of the material."

Truthfully, we never would have guessed that we would write a book, and now we are ready to send this third Cape Cod book to the publisher. This book is our ninth book covering four topics. We have written these in an attempt to share facts that we have been able to obtain about the Imperial Glass Company. It has been exciting as well as a great deal of work. We did this for the love of collecting and for the people we have met. Those people have been so appreciative of what we have attempted to do.

This work is the culmination of twenty-five years of collecting and researching Imperial Glass patterns. Many of you know that we first wrote on Imperial Cape Cod. While our collecting of Candlewick did not begin until 1978, our love of Candlewick began in 1948 when it became our wedding pattern. We have recently finished two new books on Candlewick, *Candlewick: The Crystal Line* and *Candlewick: Colored and Decorated Lines*.

Now we are pleased to have completed a third edition of *Imperial Cape Cod Glass*. We have always wanted a book with all photographs and Schiffer Publishing provided that means for us. We hope you enjoy viewing as well as learning from the results.

The words are ours unless noted otherwise and the facts are from Imperial Glass Corporation. All information compiled is from factory paper and photographs, personal collections, pictures and observations—none is based on hearsay. We appreciate the permission granted from Lancaster Colony, the last owner of the assets of Imperial, for the use and publication of photographs and documents.

Rakow Research Library of the Corning Glass Museum and the Ocean Spray Cranberries Inc. were helpful in adding information for our research. Both answered our inquiries quickly and took the time to help us.

According to Samuel Johnson, "What is written without effort is generally read without pleasure." We can say with all sincerity that this and our other books were written with very much effort!

Cape Cod factory advertising photograph that hung on the factory wall in the 1950s.

Price Guide

The prices shown represent what a knowledgeable collector would pay to a knowledgeable seller. An asterisk (*) shown for a price indicates that either none have been found or not enough have been offered for sale to establish a price. Sets are not always the sum of the parts. Neither the authors nor the publisher assume any responsibility for the pricing information herein.

Mould	Description	Dates	Price
160	8 oz. Goblet (Wafer)	1932-43	$10-12
160B	Stem Cocktail (Wafer)	1932-43	$12-15
160	Low Sherbet (Wafer)	1932-43	$10-12
160	2 1/2 oz. Wine (Wafer)	1932-43	$12-15
160	2 1/2 oz. Whiskey	1932-64	$20-22
160	6 oz. Juice Tumbler	1932-79	$12-15
160	10 oz. Water Tumbler	1940-79	$12-18
160	12 oz. Ice Tea or Highball	1932-83	$12-15
160	16 oz. Tumbler (if same as 14 oz.)	1953-73	$25-40
160	14 oz. Tumbler	1974-79	$25-40
160	7 oz. Old Fashioned	1932-78	$18-25
160	14 oz. Goblet or Ivy (Magnum)	1949-55, 1968-79	$35-45
160	36 oz. Refrigerator Jug, Open Lip	1932	$65-90
160	14 oz. Hoffman House Beer (if same as 14 oz. goblet)	1947-48	$35-45
160	14 oz. Old Fashioned, Double	1954-64, 1967-78	$25-35
160	Decanter and Stopper with name	1943	$125-140
160F	5 1/2" Compote, Cupped/Wafer Stem	1932-43	$40-55
160X	5 3/4" Compote, Flat Lip/Wafer Stem	1932-46	$40-55
160U	9 1/2" Oval Relish (160/55), Plain Lip Edge	1932-51	$30-35
160/B	Square Decanter/Stopper/Bourbon	1943	$105-115
160/G	Square Decanter/Stopper/Gin	1943	$105-115
160/R	Square Decanter/Stopper/Rye	1943	$105-115
160/S	Square Decanter/Stopped/Scotch	1943	$105-115
160/1D	6 1/2" Bread and Butter Plate	1942-82	$10-15
160/1R	4 1/2" Coaster (160/34)	1932-68	$10-15
160/1W	4 1/2" Fruit (1604W)	1932-78	$12-18
160/3D	6 3/4"-7" Plate Salad/Sherbet (1604 1/2D)	1932-78	$12-15
160/3F	6" Fruit	1954-74	$25-30
160/5D	8" Salad Plate (1606D)	1932-83	$12-15
160/5F	7" Shallow Nappy	1932-37	$35-45
160/5W	6 3/4"-7" Flared Bowl	1932-55	$25-30
160/5X	7" Bowl	1953-55	$*
160/6	Jam Spoon, 5 3/4" Long	1942	$20-25
160/7D	9" Plate	1947-64	$25-30
160/7F	7 1/2" Bowl	1951-62	$30-40
160/10D	10"-10 1/2" Dinner Plate (1602D)	1940-82	$45-55
160/10D	17" Plate Flat Edge	1932-46	$50-55
160/10D	3 pc. Buffet	1932	$65-75
160/10F	8 3/4" Bowl	1954-62	$40-50
160/12	8" Crescent Salad	1947-49	$55-70
160/19	40 oz. Ice Lip Pitcher	1947-55	$85-95
160/20	15 pc. Punch Set, 160/20B, 160/20V, 160 Cup, 160/91	1947-70	$230-295
160/20B	12" Punch Bowl, 6 Quart	1947-70	$60-75
160/20D	17"-18" Regular Edge Plate	1937-51	$50-55
160/20V	16" Cupped Plate	1937-70	$55-65
160/21	11 1/2" Footed Flip Vase	1946-51	$70-85
160/22	7 1/2" Footed Flip Vase	1947-48	$*
160/22	6 1/4" Footed Flip Vase	1951-62	$45-55
160/23/1D	2 pc. Serving Set, 160/23B, 160/1D	1974-79	$22-30
160/23	3 pc. Mayonnaise Set, 160/23B, 160/1D, #165	1946-79	$35-45
160/23B	5 1/2" Fruit (1604 1/2)	1932-79	$12-15
160/24	Ice Pitcher (2 Quarts)	1947-77	$85-95
160/25/26	Sugar, Cream and Tray Set	1947-48	$130-150
160/25	Square Sugar and Cream	1947-48	$100-110
160/26	Tray	1947-51	$30-40
160/27	6 3/4"-7" Footed Bud Vase	1947-55	$35-45
160/28	8 1/2" Footed Vase	1947-51	$45-65
160/29	7" Oblong Tray	1947-70	$18-20
160/29/30	Sugar, Cream, and Tray	1947-70	$40-50
160/30	Sugar and Cream Set	1947-82	$25-30
160/31	Footed Sugar and Cream Set, Wafer Stem (160)	1932	$30-35
160/31	Footed Sugar & Cream Set, Fancy Stem	1950-66	$35-40
160/33	3" Individual Jelly Dish (1601W)	1932-48	$12-18
160/34	4 1/2" Butter or Coaster (1601R)	1932-68	$10-15
160/35	Teacup and Saucer	1937-79	$10-12
160/35	Teacup	1937-79	$5-6
160/35	Saucer	1937-79	$5-6
160/37	Coffee Cup and Saucer	1932-82	$14-20
160/37	Coffee Cup (Punch)	1932-82	$7-10
160/37	Saucer	1932-82	$7-10
160/40	Handled Basket, Height 11", Flat Bottom	1947-62	$*
160/40	Handled Basket, Height 11", Footed Bottom	????	$145-160
160/40H	6" Handled Heart	1954-62, 1977-79	$20-30
160/45	6" Comporte, Footed	1947-62	$30-35
160/45B	5" Flower Candleholder	1947-51	$75-95
160/45N	5 1/2" Candleholder	1947-51	$85-110
160/48B	6" Flower Candle Centerpiece	1947-51	$95-125
160/48B	7" Footed Comporte	1947-62	$35-45
160/49H	5" Heart Shape, Mint or Dessert	1947-64	$20-30
160/51F	6" Round Handled Mint	1954-64	$30-35
160/51H	6" Handled Heart Tray	1954-62	$30-35
160/51T	6" Handled Heart Tray	1954-64	$25-30
160/52D	7" Plate, Mayonnaise Under Plate	1947-62	$15-20
160/52H	3 pc. Mayonnaise Set, 160/52B, 49H Heart, 52D Plate, 165 Ladle	1947-62	$50-60
160/53/3	3 pc. Icer Set, 160/53B, #530 Sherbet, #530 Tumbler	1953-55	$85-100
160/53B	Icer, 3 Interior Wedges	1953-55	$35-40
160/53X	6" Baked Apple (1604 1/2X)	1932-78	$10-15
160/55	9 1/2" Oval Relish, Plain Edge (160U)	1932-51	$30-35
160/55	9 1/2" Oval Relish, Designed Edge	1953-79	$30-35
160/56	9 1/2" Relish, Four Divided, Handles	1947-78	$35-40

Mould	Description	Dates	Price
160/61	Salt Dip	1947-62	$20-22
160/62B	7 1/2" Two Handled Bowl (1602B)	1942-79	$25-35
160/62D	8 1/2" Two Handled Plate	1947-64	$30-40
160/62D	9 1/2" Two Handled Plate (1602D)	1942-46	$*
160/63	6 1/2" Ice Bucket and Tongs	1947-48	$200-225
160/67D	10 1/2" Footed Cake Stand, Flat	1947-79	$60-70
160/67F	9" Footed Fruit Bowl	1947-64	$70-80
160/68D	11" Pastry Tray Center Handled	1953-64	$110-125
160/70	5 oz. Cruet and Stopper, Pointed Stopper	1942-77	$30-32
160/70	5 oz. Cruet and Stopper, Fancy Stopper	1978-82	$25-30
160/72	72 Candle Plate 13" (Tradition)	1932-51, 1954, 1983	$125-135
160/72	72 Candle Plate 13" (Cape Cod)	????	$300-325
160/73/0	11" Basket, Oval	1947-51	$200-225
160/75	4 pc. Salad Set (1608/4) 160/75B, 160/75V, #701	1942-69	$95-115
160/75B	12" Bowl (1608B 11")	1937-69	$30-35
160/75D	14" Flat Plate (1608D)	1943-79	$25-40
160/75L	13" Center Bowl	1941-51	$40-50
160/75V	14" Cupped Plate (1608V)	1942-71	$40-45
160/76	Coaster With Spoon Rest	1950-82	$12-15
160/78	4" Coaster, Round	1947-68	$15-20
160/79	2 pc. Hurricane Lamp	1947-55, 1977-80	$110-130
160/79	5" Candle Base	1947-55, 1977-80	$60-70
160/79	Chimney	1947-55, 1977-80	$50-60
160/80	5" Candleholder	1941-69, 1974-79	$25-30
160/80/2	Eagle Candleholder	1943-50	$250-275
160/81	4" Candleholder	1947-51	$30-35
160/82	16 oz. Cordial Bottle	1947-48	$190-210
160/85	3" Square Coaster	1955-68	$22-25
160/87F	8" Fan Vase	1947-47	$200-225
160/88	2 pc. Cheese and Cracker (No Picture in Catalogs)	1954-56	$*
160/89	4 pc. Marmalade Set, 160/89, 160/6, 160/37, 160/130	1942-64	$47-57
160/89/3	3 pc. Marmalade Set, 160/89, 160/6, 160/37	1947-64	$35-45
160/90	4" Handled Aladdin Candleholder	1951	$120-135
160/91	Punch Ladle	1938-70	$30-35
160/92F	14"-14 1/2" Center Bowl, Float Bowl	1942-51	$50-65
160/93	12" Multi Server	1954-62	$80-90
160/94	5" Deep Mayonnaise, Wide Plain Band (AKA 1600J)	1932-46	$40-50
160/94	3 pc. Buffet, 16010V (AKA 160/94V), 1600J, 160/165	1947-51	$110-130
160/96	Salt and Pepper Set	1942-73	$20-25
160/100	Twin Candleholder	1947-62	$60-75
160/100	2 Lite Candleholder and Ornament, Removable	1947-48	$*
160/102	11" 5 Part Relish	1946-62	$55-70
160/103D	11" Cake Stand, Apron, Plain Top	1947-53	$115-135
160/103D	11" Cake Stand, Pattern Top	1954-62	$90-100
160/105	8" Celery Dish, Oval	1953-64	$40-50
160/109	Square Salt and Pepper	1947-51	$25-30
160/110	10" Footed Candy Jar, 1 lb. Covered	1947-62	$65-75
160/110B	6 1/2" Footed Vase	1947-48	$75-85
160/116	Footed Salt and Pepper Set	1943-78	$25-35
160/117	Shaker	1968-82	$12-15
160/119	4 oz. Cruet and Stopper	1950-82	$25-30
160/120	14 pc. Punch Bowl Set 160/120, 160/37, 160/91	1947-48	$365-440

Mould	Description	Dates	Price
160/120B	Punch Bowl, Footed	1947-48	$250-295
160/123	Covered Toast, Butter or Cheese	1947-51	$*
160/124	11" Oval Vegetable Bowl	1942-51	$80-95
160/124D	13 1/2" Platter Oval	1942-51	$50-60
160/125	11" Oval Partitioned Vegetable	1947-48	$85-95
160/128	11" Covered Jar, Pokal	1947-51	$70-85
160/130	Ladle, 2 Bead	1947-70	$15-20
160/131B	12" Oval Center Bowl	1947-55	$90-100
160/131C	12" Oval Crimped Bowl	1953-64	$80-95
160/132	15" Covered Pokal	1947-51	$135-150
160/133	10" Covered Pokal	1947-48	$120-140
160/134	4 1/2" Handled Cigarette Box and Cover	1947-57	$35-45
160/134/1	4" Ash Tray, Single Rest	1947-64	$15-20
160/134/6	6 pc. Cigarette Set, Box, 4 Ash Trays	1947-55	$95-125
160/137B	10" Footed Bowl, Shallow	1947-62	$70-85
160/140	6" Covered Footed Comporte	1947-62	$55-65
160/143	8 1/2" Flip Vase (1602)	1942-55	$60-75
160/144	5" Handled Butter and Cover	1947-68, 1977-78	$35-50
160/145B	9 1/2"-10", 2-Handled Bowl	1947-78	$45-55
160/145D	11 1/2" 2-Handled Plate	1947-78	$40-50
160/149D	8" Center Handled Tray	1953-62	$115-130
160/150	5 1/2" Ashtray, Double Rest	1947-57, 1977	$20-25
160/156	Covered Mustard and Spoon	1947-64	$55-70
160/157	5 pc. Condiment Set, Pointed Stopper, 160/55, 160/70, 160/116	1947-51	$110-130
160/157	5 pc. Condiment Set, Round Stopper, 160/55, 160/70, 160/116	1951-64	$115-125
160/161	Oblong Butter and Cover	1953-67, 1977-82	$40-50
160/163	30 oz. Decanter and Stopper	1932-64	$55-65
160/165	Ladle, Mayonnaise, One Bead	1948-70	$12-18
160/170	3" Single Candleholder	1953-62	$20-25
160/175	4 1/2" Saucer Candle (1604W)	1932-43, 1953-62	$40-45
160/176	80 oz. Blown Pitcher, 5 Pint	1947-64, 1977-79	$150-175
160/177	4 oz. Oil Cruet and Stopper	1947-55	$30-35
160/178	40 oz. Blown Martini Pitcher	1947-55	225-250
160/180	4 1/2" Handled Spider	1947-79	$25-35
160/181	5 1/2" Handled Spider	1947-74	$25-35
160/182	6 1/2" Handled Spider	1947-48	$40-45
160/183	3" Handled Nut or Mint	1947-69	$25-30
160/184	4" Handled Nut or Mint	1947-51	$30-35
160/185	Wine Carafe, 26 oz. and Stopper	1947-48	$185-200
160/186	10 1/2" 2-Handled Urn Vase	1947-48	$140-160
160/187	6 1/2" Handled Partitioned Spider	1947-64	$40-45
160/188	12 oz. Handled Stein	1947-51	$55-65
160/189	10 1/2" Celery Tray	1947-51	$55-65
160/190	Sugar and Creamer, Footed	1954-61	$*
160/191	10 1/2" Partitioned Relish (1/2 x 1/2)	1947-48	$*
160/191	10 1/2" Partitioned Relish (1/3 x 2/3)	????	$75-95
160/192	10" Cylinder Vase	1947-62	$135-150
160/192	8 1/2" Partitioned Peanut & Mint	1947	$175-195
160/193	3 1/2" x 4" Peanut Jar, Handled	1947-51	$115-130
160/194	4 1/2" x 5" Candy Jar, Handled	1947-48	$130-145
160/195	6 1/4" x 6 1/2" Cookie Jar, Handled	1947-48	$170-200
160/196	2 pc. Epergne	1947-55	$180-200
160/197	4 1/2" Lug Dessert	1947-48	$35-45
160/198	5 1/2" Lug Soup	1947-51, 1982	$25-35
160/199	6 1/2" Lug Bowl	1947-48	$35-45
160/200	Handled Cigarette Holder or Tom and Jerry Mug	1947-51	$50-65
160/200	14 pc. Tom and Jerry Set, 160/120B, 160/200	1947-48	$800-950

Mould	Description	Dates	Price
160/201	18 oz. Gravy Bowl, 8" Cupped Plate Set	1947-48	$105-125
160/202	18 oz. Gravy Bowl	1947-51	$50-60
160/203	8" Cupped Plate	1947-48	$55-65
160/204	12 oz. Mayonnaise Bowl, 7" Cupped Plate Set	1947-48	$100-120
160/205	12 oz. Mayonnaise Bowl	1947-51	$50-60
160/206	7" Cupped Plate	1947-48	$50-60
160/207	6 oz. Salad Dressing, 6" Cupped Plate Set	1947-48	$100-120
160/208	6 oz. Salad Dressing Bowl	1947-48	$50-60
160/209	6" Cupped Plate	1947-48	$50-60
160/210	Handled Peanut Jar and Cover	1947-51	$90-110
160/211	Tray, Salt	1947-51	$15-25
160/212	24 oz. Decanter and Stopper, Square	1946-64	$65-75
160/213	3 pc. Salt, Pepper and Tray, 160/96, 160/183	1947-69	$45-55
160/216	3 pc. Salt, Pepper and Tray, 160/116, 160/184	1947-51	$55-65
160/219	3 pc. Salt Dip, 160/109, 1600 Salt Spoon, 160/211	1947-51	$40-70
160/220	10" 4-Toed Cake Stand	1947-62	$70-80
160/221	10" Oval Bowl, Vegetable	1947-51	$175-190
160/221C	9 1/2" Crimped Bowl	1953-62	$215-235
160/221F	9 1/2" Float Bowl	1953-62	$75-100
160/221/0	9" Handled Basket	1953-64	$170-190
160/222	12 1/2" Bread Plate	1947-48	$70-85
160/223	Partitioned Cigarette Server	1947-51	$40-55
160/223	8 1/2" Handled Partitioned Server	1951-59	$40-55
160/224	6 oz. Condiment Bottle and Tube	1947-55	$45-55
160/225	Egg Cup	1947-62	$30-35
160/226	Horseradish Jar, 5 oz.	1947-51	$75-90
160/228	9 pc. Footed Water Set, 160/24, 1602, 10 oz.	1947-66	$180-215
160/229	9 pc. Footed Juice Set, 160/19, 40 oz.; 1602, Ftd. Juice	1947-55	$180-215
160/230	9 pc. Water Set, 160/24, 160, 10 oz. Ftd. Tumbler	1947-66	$180-240
160/232	9 pc. Footed Wine Set, 160/185, 1602 Wine	1947-48	$280-320
160/233	9 pc. Cordial Set, 160/82, 1602 Cordial	1947-48	$280-330
160/235	4 oz. Bitter and Tube	1947-55	$50-55
160/236	Pepper Mill	1947-48	$25-35
160/237	14 oz. Ketchup, Wooden Lid	1947-48	$*
160/237	14 oz. Ketchup, Chrome Lid	????	$*
160/238	Salt Shaker	1947-48	$20-25
160/239	Ice Pitcher, 2 Quart Lipped	1947-62	$80-90
160/240	Milk Pitcher, Pint	1947-73	$45-55
160/241	6 oz. Oil, Vinegar & Pointed Stopper	1947-52	$40-45
160/241	6 oz. Oil, Vinegar & Round Stopper	1953-55	$40-45
160/242	5 1/2" Tray	1947-51	$20-22
160/243	Footed Salt and Pepper	1947-64	$40-50
160/244	26 oz. Bar Bottle and Stopper	1947-64	$125-145
160/246	Square Pitcher (Mould Scrapped 1948)	1948	$*
160/247	Salt and Pepper	1947-48	$45-50
160/250	Bouillon Cup	1947-51	$50-55
160/251	Individual Salt and Pepper Set, Round	1947-82	$20-25
160/252	Covered Ketchup and Spoon	1947-51	$40-50
160/256	18 oz. Cordial Bottle and Stopper	1947-51	$175-190
160/260	Decanter, Square, Scotch, Bourbon, Rye	1955-64	$95-110
160/455	7" Square Tray	1953-55	$170-180
160/459	5 pc. Condiment Set, 160/119, 160/116	1953-55	$245-290
160/822	3 pc. Cottage Console Set, 160/221, 160/81	1947-51	$235-260
160/1112	4 pc. Relish Set, 160/130	1947-61	$125-150
160/1630	7 pc. Wine Set, 160/163, 1602 Wine	1932-64	$127-155
160/1639	7 pc. Whiskey Set, 160/163, 160 Whiskey	1932-64	$175-200
160/1971	4 1/2" Blown Pepper Mill and Salt Shaker	1971-74	$115-135
160/2120	7 pc. Whiskey Set, 160/212, 160 Whiskey	1947-64	$185-205
160/2368	Salt and Pepper Tray Set, 160/236, 160/238, 160/242	1947-48	$65-80
160/2426	3 pc. Oil and Vinegar, 160/241, 160/26	1947-51	$110-130
160/2701	2-Tier Tidbit Set, Wood, Later Wire	1943, 1953-55	$*
160/2941	3 pc. Oil and Vinegar, 160/241, 160/29	1947-48	$95-110
160/5629	3 pc. Mustard and Ketchup, 160/156, 160/29	1947-64	$115-140
160/7724	3 pc. Oil and Vinegar, 160/177, 160/242	1947-51	$80-90
160/8075B	3 pc. Console Set, 160/75B, 160/80	1948-48	$80-95
160/8075L	3 pc. Console Set, 160/75L, 160/80	1942-51	$90-110
160/8092F	3 pc. Console Set, 160/92F, 160/80	1942-51	$115-135
160/8137	3 pc. Console Set, 160/137B, 160/81	1947-51	$130-155
1600	10 oz. Goblet	1947-68	$25-30
1600	6 oz. Sherbet	1947-68	$25-30
1600	12 oz. Footed Ice Tea Tumbler	1947-68	$25-30
1600	6 oz. Footed Juice Tumbler	1947-51	$30-35
1600	3 oz. Wine	1947-51	$35-40
1600	3 1/2 oz. Cocktail	1947-51	$30-35
1600	Salt Spoon	1953-58	$15-20
1600D	7" Mayonnaise Plate (AKA 160/1D)	1937-43	$10-12
1600J	5" Deep Mayonnaise (AKA 160/94)	1932-46	$40-50
1601	12 oz. Ice Tea Tumbler	1951-51	$35-45
1601	9 oz. Water Tumbler	1951-51	$35-45
1601	6 oz. Juice Tumbler	1951-51	$35-45
1601	Dresser Set 6 pc., 1601 Colognes (2), 1601 Powder Box	1932-46	$195-235
1601	Cologne, Stopper	1932-46	$60-70
1601	Powder Box	1932-46	$75-95
1601R	Coaster, 4 1/2" (AKA 160/34)	1932-68	$10-15
1602	9 oz. Luncheon Goblet	1942-74	$10-12
1602	11 oz. Dinner Goblet	1942-83	$12-15
1602	6 oz. Tall Sherbet or Saucer Champagne	1942-79	$10-15
1602	6 oz. Low Sundae	1942-83	$10-12
1602	3 1/2 oz. Cocktail	1942-73	$10-12
1602	1 1/2 oz. Cordial	1946-73	$12-15
1602	3 oz. Wine	1942-74	$12-15
1602	5 oz. Claret or Wine	1942-83	$12-15
1602	2 1/2 oz. Sherry	1951-51	$50-75
1602	6 oz. Parfait	1951-74	$12-18
1602	6 oz. Footed Juice Tumbler	1942-76	$12-15
1602	6 oz. Footed Juice Tumbler, Concave Stem	1940-42	$30-40
1602	10 oz. Footed Tumbler	1946-73	$12-15
1602	12 oz. Footed Ice Tea Tumbler	1942-83	$15-20
1602	12 oz. Footed Ice Tea Concave Stem	1940-42	$30-40
1602	4 oz. Oyster or Fruit Cocktail	1942-71	$15-20
1602	4 oz. Oyster or Fruit Cocktail, Concave Stem	1940-42	$30-40
1602	Finger Bowl	1947-74	$12-15
1602	Salt and Pepper, Plastic Lids (AKA 160/96)	1942-42	$25-30
1602	Cigarette Lighter	1962-66	$40-50
1602	Footed Cigarette Holder (AKA Oyster Cocktail)	1949-70	$15-20
1602	6 1/2" x 11 1/4" Footed Oval Compote	1942-43	$*

Mould	Description	Dates	Price
1602	11 1/4" Shallow Vegetable Bowl, Oval	1942-43	$90-100
1602	11 1/4" Three Part Relish, Oval	1942-43	$90-100
1603	11" Flip Vase, Straight Sides	1942-43	$*
1604	2 pc. Hurricane Lamp	1942-46	$140-160
1604 1/2A	4 1/2" Finger Bowl	1932-46	$12-15
1604 1/2B	5 1/2" Belled Fruit	1932-43	$15-20
1604 1/2B	3 pc. Mayonnaise, 160/23B, 1600D, #615	1937-43	$35-45
1604W	Saucer Candleholder	1932-43	$40-45
1605	3 pc. Mayonnaise Set, 160/23B, 160/1D, 160/165	1932-32	$35-45
1605N	5" Cupped Flower Bowl	1932-43	$*
1608A	11" Round Bowl, 1/2" Plain Edge	1932-37	$100-125
1608B	11" Salad Bowl	1940-43	$30-35
1608D	14" Flat Plate	1943-46	$25-40
1608F	13 1/2" Torte Plate (AKA 160/75F)	1932-32	$25-40
1608L	Console Bowl	1942-43	$40-55
1608V	13 1/2" Cupped Plate (AKA 160/75V)	1932-43	$40-45
1608X	11"-11 1/2" Bowl, Flanged Edge	1932-32	$*
16010	15 pc. Punch Bowl Set	1932-46	$225-250
16010A	11" Salad Bowl, 1 1/2" Plain Edge	1932-38	$*
16010B	12 1/2" Punch Bowl	1932-46	$35-65
16010B	12 1/2" Fruit Bowl Bell Shaped, 1 1/2" Plain Edge	1932-43	$*
16010D	10" Dinner Plate	1940-82	$45-55
16010D	17" Plate Flat Edge	1932-46	$45-55
16010D	3 pc. Buffet Set, 160/20D, 1600J, #615	1932-65	$115-140
16010L	15" Center Bowl, Wide Plain Edge	1942-46	$*
16010 1F	5 pc. Console, 160/92F, 1601 Candleholder	1942-46	$*
16010 1L	5 pc. Console, 16010L Center Bowl, 1601 Candleholder	1942-46	$*
16010R	13" Center Bowl	1932-37	$*
16010V	16" Plate, Cupped Edge	1932-46	$60-65
16010V	3 pc. Buffet Set, 16010V, 1600J, #615	1932-46	$110-130
3600	11 oz. Goblet, Blown	1951-57	$35-45
3600	6 oz. Sherbet, Blown	1951-57	$35-45
3600	4 oz. Cocktail, Blown	1951-57	$35-45
3600	5 oz. Wine, Blown	1951-57	$35-45
3600	1 1/2 oz. Cordial, Blown	1951-57	$*
3600	6 oz. Juice Tumbler, Blown	1951-57	$35-45
3600	12 oz. Ice Tea Tumbler, Blown	1951-57	$35-45
3611	5 oz. Footed Tumbler	1953-55	$*
3612	12 oz. Footed Tumbler	1953-55	$*
16880	Spider Candleholder, Raised Ring in Center	1974-75	$55-75
#165	54 oz. Ice Jug (Tradition Pattern)	1932-43	$50-60
#530	Sherbet Lining	1953-55	$25-30
#530	5 1/2 oz. Tumbler	1953-55	$25-30
#615	Ladle, Plain	1932-46	$10-15
#701	Fork and Spoon Set (Reeded Pattern)	1932-68	$25-35
#701	Muddler (Reeded Pattern)	1932-37	$20-25

Bibliography

A Consumer and Retail Guide to Handcrafted Glassware. Imperial Booklet. Bellaire, OH: Imperial Glass Corp.

Garrison, Myrna and Bob. *Imperial Cape Cod: Tradition to Treasure*, Self-Published, ©1992.

Garrison, Myrna and Bob. *Imperial's Boudoir, Etcetera.* Self-Published, © 1996.

Stout, Sandra McPhee. *The Complete Book of McKee Glass.* North Kansas City, Missouri: Trojan Press, Inc., 1972.

Lee, Ruth Webb. *Early American Pressed Glass, Enlarged and Revised.* Wellesley Hills, Massachusetts: Lee Publication, 1960.

Taylor, Dorothy. *Carnival Glass Encore*. Kansas City, Missouri: circa 1970s.

Quoted material came from notes, advertising books, memorandums, price lists and other paper documents from the defunct Imperial Glass Corporation, Bellaire, Ohio 43906, 1901-1984.

Index